THE
MARTIAL
ARTS
AND
REAL LIFE

THE MARTIAL ARTS AND REAL LIFE

A Book of Fighting for the Twenty-first Century

FRED VILLARI

QUILL
New York

Library of Congress Cataloging in Publication Data

Villari, Fred.
  The martial arts and real life.

  Includes index.
  1. Hand-to-hand fighting.   2. Self-defense.
I. Title.
GV1111.V54   1985b   796.8   85-504
ISBN 0-688-05248-7
ISBN 0-688-04714-9 (pbk)

Printed in the United States of America

        8 9 10

BOOK DESIGN BY RICHARD ORIOLO

To my late father, Frederick Joseph Villari, who was mainly responsible for influencing me and introducing me to the fascinating and exciting arts of fighting.

To my wife Joan and my children for their encouragement and their faith in me.

ACKNOWLEDGMENT

I wish to express my gratitude to Joan Choo Chong Villari for her splendid assistance in the preparation of this book.

CONTENTS

INTRODUCTION

This book will not teach you the magic of the martial arts. It will not reveal to you the secrets of karate, and it will not turn you into an awesome street fighter overnight.

There is no magic. The martial arts have no more secrets than tenpin bowling. And if your goal is to learn how to flip two thugs over a parked car by next Saturday afternoon, you're wasting your time with this book.

Karate, kung fu, and the other self-defense methods we'll discuss have survived for centuries because they are based on practical and logical principles. There is nothing magical about them, and you don't need special wisdom or insight to learn them. What you do need is curiosity, enthusiasm, humility, dedication, and discipline. In the martial arts competence does not come easily and mastery does not come often, but you can achieve both if you want to. So if you're looking for a method of self-defense that comes quickly and easily, I suggest you buy a can of mace; this book is not for you. But this book is for everybody else.

It is for the guy who has been enjoying the physical benefits of the martial arts for years, but has never given much thought to the mental aspects of the arts. It is for the woman who is shocked and alarmed at the growing number of crimes directed toward women and wants to know how she can protect herself. It is for the honest and hardworking man who has never hurt anybody, but leaves the factory every night scared because he has to walk across a dark parking lot. And it is for the teenaged boy or girl who needs to gain peace of mind and confidence, who wants to master some skill that he or she can be proud of.

So this book is for you, whether you are young or old, man

or woman, fourth-degree black belt or novice. I hope I can speed the progress of the beginner and expand the knowledge of the veteran martial artist. Take from this book only what works for you, and leave the rest behind.

In saying that this book is for everybody, I guess I sound like a missionary for the martial arts, but I really believe that martial-arts training would benefit everybody. Certainly only a small minority of us will ever have to unleash a self-defense technique against a mugger. But all of us seek good health, energy, and peace, and the martial arts are an efficient and exciting path to those goals.

I have tried to keep the book general, emphasizing the principles rather than specific situations that might come up for you. But I have included some specific techniques to get you started and to give you the flavor of the activity. Keep in mind, however, that the ideal way to learn technique is through intelligent, open-minded personal instruction. A book can start you on your martial-arts journey, but it is difficult to learn techniques through a book because your intellectual book-reading mind does not learn them; your body does. The book can tell your mind what to tell your body, but then the body has to practice. So you will eventually need a skilled instructor.

The place where you study the martial arts is a *dojo*. Traditionally, the *dojo* is called "the place of enlightenment." There is a Buddhist saying that any place can be a *dojo*, so I suppose that means a book can be a *dojo*, too, and I hope that this book will be for you a place of enlightenment.

I

ENTER THE *DOJO*

THE FIGHTING PREMISE

Throughout this book I will refer often to "fighting," or "when you are attacked," or "your opponent." But I don't want you to get the idea that I expect you to be mugged next week on your way home from the movies, or attacked by some lunatic who goes berserk in the 7-Eleven. I don't. I talk about fighting because the possibility that you will be attacked is the basic premise in all martial-arts training.

Take, for example, a guy who joins the local police force. He is given a pistol and everybody hopes like hell that he will never have to use it. But the gun is given to him on the assumption that someday he might be staring into the barrel of somebody else's gun and that he might have to shoot. So they teach him how to use his pistol effectively; in other words, how to shoot and even kill people with it.

It's the same with the martial arts. One premise behind all martial-arts training is that someday you are going to have to use it. And you're going to have to use it *effectively,* not just for show. Someday there might be a bully with a knife, or a thug, or a rapist, or just some dangerously insane person, and you are going to have to immobilize him at the very least, maybe injure him so that he can't come at you again, or maybe kill him.

I hope that day never comes. And I hope that you survive if it does come. A knowledge of the martial arts is the best insurance policy you could have. Remember that if there were no weirdos and bullies who wanted to hurt people with knives, guns, and clubs, the martial arts might never have come into existence. And remember also that even if you never have to use your weapon, the peace of mind that comes with knowing you have it if you need it is well worth the time and effort you put into studying the arts.

It's not enough simply to hurt an attacker. Your goal is to immobilize him so that he can't come at you again.

So when I talk about "your attacker" or "the fight you're in," don't worry. I have no crystal ball. I speak to you in those terms only because that confrontation, that fight, is a spot in the distance on which you should focus throughout your martial-arts training.

So view the martial arts as a path to inner peace, if that's what you choose to do. Regard it as a sport, as a way to lose weight, as a physical-fitness discipline, or simply as something to do. All of these are fine. But keep your eye on that imaginary confrontation, that spot in the distance, and let it guide you through all of your training in the martial arts. I want you to see fighting as both a literal possibility and a metaphor for battles with any enemy you have in mind, whether it's obesity, stress, laziness, or a street mugger.

TWO STORIES ABOUT A DWARF

Several hundred years ago in Lombardy, a section of northern Italy, there lived a dwarf by the name of Rustico Bertholde. Bertholde was a plucky little character and legend has it that when he reached a certain age and knew that jobs for dwarves were hard to come by, he went directly to the king to ask for a job. The king was having a merry time entertaining a bunch of noblemen and courtiers. When Bertholde was brought before them they all started to laugh and make dwarf jokes. Bertholde was irate, and he reprimanded the whole crew. He said that the king, especially, should be ashamed of himself for making fun of the handicapped.

The king, apparently, did not take criticism well, because he ordered his soldiers to take Bertholde out and hang him for his insolence. The dwarf asked to be granted one last wish, which was customary at the time. The king asked what it was and Bertholde said he would like to choose the hanging tree. That seemed pretty reasonable; so the king said fine and told his soldiers to take Bertholde away.

A few hours later the soldiers returned. They still had Bertholde with them, and they looked exasperated.

"What's the problem?" the king asked.

"Well, sir," replied one of the soldiers, "the dwarf has picked his tree."

17

"So?"

"It's only two feet high," the soldier said. "But he says he's willing to wait for it to grow."

The story is that the king was so impressed by Bertholde's genius that he appointed the dwarf as prime minister of Lombardy.

Some time later the king was murdered, the arrangements having been made by his wife, the queen. Bertholde discovered the wretched queen's secret, and when she found out that he knew, she decided he would have to be knocked off, too.

The queen schemed to have her palace guard dogs, two enormous mastiffs, unleashed so they could attack and kill Bertholde. But Bertholde caught wind of the plan; he knew when and where it was supposed to happen, and he was ready. As he came out of his office one morning and started to walk down the palace corridors, the queen's guards released the dogs. These huge vicious mutts came loping and snarling down the corridor after the dwarf, and when the mastiffs got close, Bertholde threw open his coat and released a rabbit. The rabbit scurried down the corridor, the dogs chased the rabbit, and Bertholde went about his business.

"Well, gee, that's real interesting," you're probably saying by now, "but what has it got to do with the martial arts?" The answer is "A lot."

As far as I know, Bertholde was not a practitioner of the martial arts. And I know for a fact that he never enrolled at Fred Villari's Studios of Self-Defense. But he had wisdom and self-assurance, essential qualities for the successful martial artist, and in these situations he demonstrated a number of principles that should guide you in the martial arts.

1. DEVELOP THE MIND.
   Bertholde did not have strength, speed, height, or great weight, his balance was probably lousy, and he had no training. But he effectively used the martial artist's greatest weapon, the mind.
2. LOOK AT THE SOLUTION, NOT THE PROBLEM.
   Bertholde did not take a self-defeating attitude. He worked on a way to defeat his enemies.
3. IF IT WORKS, IT'S GOOD.

Though he did not use any fancy weapons or fighting techniques, he outsmarted his enemies. That worked for him. It saved his life.

4. BE CONFIDENT.
   He believed in himself. He was confident of his ability to survive and upset his opponents' plans to kill him.

5. ELIMINATE FEAR.
   Bertholde knew that fear could destroy him. He did away with fear and acted in a calm, rational manner at the crucial moments.

6. USE YOUR OPPONENT.
   Bertholde found his opponents' weaknesses and used it against them. In the incident with the dogs, he knew they had a weakness for chasing rabbits, so he used that weakness to save his own life.

7. USE YOUR STRENGTHS.
   He knew that he could not overpower soldiers and huge snarling dogs, so he used his sharp wits, his strength, to outsmart them.

We'll be discussing all of these principles as we go along. But for now I just want to point out that all of them were used by a man who had no training and none of the physical attributes we commonly associate with successful fighting. Everyone has some shortcoming, some handicap, but whatever yours is, it doesn't have to prevent you from progressing and achieving superiority in the martial arts. You can start to become a good martial artist right now, long before you enter a training studio, simply by developing your mind and your spirit. I hope this book will help.

THE FIGHTING SYSTEMS

When we talk about fighting systems, people usually think first of karate. But fighting systems don't stop there. In China there are Shaolin kempo, wu-shu, and kung fu. In Japan and Okinawa, besides karate, there are aikido, judo, and jujitsu. In the U.S.A. we have our own forms of unarmed combat. I'm not talking about pro football; I mean boxing and wrestling.

19

If there are some unfriendly creatures waiting for you in the parking lot when you come out from your first visit to a *dojo*, I don't advise you to try this. But don't underestimate your potential. All the skills of the martial artist are there for you to learn, and you can start to become a good martial artist right now, by developing your mind and your spirit.

Many of the Asian fighting systems have their roots in the Chinese Shaolin temple. However, over the centuries, the martial or fighting arts have been enriched by many cultures and many people, and traditionally they have been interwoven with philosophy and matters of the spirit. Through the years, wise innovations, personal prejudices, unique situations, and plain old stubbornness have combined to create a variety of martial-arts systems. There are main systems, and each has subdivisions. Kung fu, for example, has hundreds of subdivisions. The systems have different origins, different founders, and different moves that are considered to be essential. Some are linear: Most of the moves go in a straight line. Some are circular: The movement of the combatants tend toward arcs and circles. The number of different systems is enough to make you want to turn in your karate uniform and take up softball. But don't worry about the plethora of martial-arts systems. You only need to know one: The one that works for you.

I favor the Shaolin kempo system because it is strictly a devastating method of combat. At my schools we teach this fighting system, which evolved in China about four thousand years ago. It is based on the movements of five animals and is a fighting method consisting of extremely powerful techniques for delivering blows and kicks. These tactics were used by the Shaolin fighters who made quite a name for themselves in this ancient art. Like most martial-arts systems, Shaolin kempo was developed by people who had few weapons other than their own bodies and knew they were going to get clobbered by someone else's well-equipped army unless they developed their bodies and minds into formidable fighting weapons. And, like most martial-arts systems, Shaolin kempo grew from being simply a weapon of self-defense to being a physical and spiritual discipline, a way of life.

So Shaolin kempo is the one true martial art, right? Wrong. For me it is just the basis of what I do. It is the fundamental structure on which I build my system. If there's a technique that won't work because it's not right for me, the situation, or the opponent, I get rid of it. If I've found something new that is right and will work, I include it. My system of fighting is a system that works. I've been immersed in the fighting arts for over three decades and I've discovered the precise strengths and weaknesses of the art of fighting.

Because the fighting systems date back to antiquity, many people get stuck in the old system. They become dogmatic, inflexible. Certainly we should revere and respect the old ways, but we also must be practical and flexible so that we can adapt our fighting techniques to the real situations of today. Many fighting systems contain techniques that are not practical for today. This book is geared toward realistic fighting in modern times.

There are two important points I want to stress about fighting systems:

The first is relax. Don't worry because you think there will be one system that you know and 723 that you don't know. The similarities far outnumber the differences, and the fundamentals apply to all systems.

The second is don't worry about whether you are being trained in the right system. If any martial-arts instructor tells you he's teaching you the "one true system," get another instructor or you'll be studying under an idiot. The idea of the one true system is foisted off on students only by instructors of limited knowledge who need to feel important.

The only good system is the one that works for you, and it will probably be a combination of fighting techniques taken from many systems. It also might include some sharp moves that have never appeared in any system before because they came directly from your mind. After you have mastered the principles and reached a high level of expertise, you will learn many things from yourself. Search deep within your own mind and you will discover the secrets of the fighting arts. The only good technique is a technique that gets the job done. If a technique doesn't work for you, don't waste your time on it. *The system should be your servant, not your master.* Never subscribe to the narrow-minded notion that if something is not in your system it is no good. Too many martial artists put too much emphasis on their system, and this contributes to the stagnation of their martial-arts skills.

A lot of martial-arts teachers are inflexible in their thinking. They get hung up on a system and can't see beyond it. They believe, for example, in a wholly linear system, so they teach their students only how to come straight in, attack, and punch or kick, hoping that one blow will defeat the opponent.

The only good technique is the technique that works.

This is wrong. The instructor is building his system on the shaky premise that the student will only be fighting guys who went to the same school. What if the student comes up against a 280-pound unorthodox fighter who's not in the mood to play dead after just one blow? A guy like that might have to be hit four or five times, and even then the student might have to take him off his feet and go to work on him on the ground. And if techniques for that are not in the student's system, then he'd better be a fast runner or know some effective prayers. A system that does not contain techniques for every situation is almost worthless, because all your opponent has to do is create the situation that you are not equipped to deal with.

The wise teacher and the curious student should always be open to ideas from all systems and should be willing to draw from those systems any technique that is compatible, natural, and workable. When the system is right you can feel it. You shed all the things that are uncomfortable to do. It's as natural as walking down the street. You move easily, you feel your power and balance, and you know you can deal with any situation. That's the kind of system that this book is about. Effective fighting, fighting that works in real-life situations.

II

MENTAL PRINCIPLES

MEDITATION

The ancient practice of meditation is a vital element in mastering the fighting arts. Millions of people throughout the world practice meditation for improved health and spiritual peace. It is valuable not only to students of the martial arts, but also to students in general. It leads you to a quiet and receptive state of mind in which you can learn and retain information more easily. For the martial artist, meditation should be mandatory.

Besides increasing creativity and the ability to learn, meditation can increase alertness and energy, and decrease anxiety, boredom, stress, insomnia, and the craving for drugs, alcohol, and cigarettes.

Everyone can benefit from meditation. I'm not revealing any secrets when I tell you that pressure and stress can kill. All of us have known people with ulcers and a two-pack-a-day habit. And we have all heard of someone who died suddenly of a heart attack one afternoon at the office. The report of the death is always followed by something like "And he was only fifty-two. That's not old." That's true, and it doesn't have to happen to you. So the martial arts in conjunction with meditation will increase your ability to handle pressure and stress. It will help you to react calmly and appropriately in pressure situations. The greater the obstacle you face, the better you will perform. You will learn to control pressure and it will bring out the best in your natural abilities.

HOW TO MEDITATE

Just as there are people who offer the one true martial-arts system, the streets are thick with charlatans who want to sell you the one true way to meditate. There is no one true way. There are many ways to meditate, and here I will discuss one that I favor. It works for me.

Keep in mind that you don't have to do anything extreme or bizarre in order to meditate successfully. You don't have to hide in a cave or sit silently on top of a mountain for five years. You don't have to live on brown rice and bean sprouts, turn yourself into a human pretzel, or sack out on a bed of nails in order to earn the benefits of meditation. Keep it simple. Make it part of your daily life. You should meditate fifteen to thirty minutes a day, either first thing in the morning, or perhaps in the early evening. You can meditate on a train, in the bathtub, or in a quiet room at home, wherever you feel comfortable and won't be interrupted.

Find a quiet, comfortable place and sit. If you are comfortable in the traditional posture—legs crossed and open hands resting on knees—then fine. If you're more comfortable with your feet up on a hassock and your hands on your lap, then do it that way. Don't try to do anything immediately. Just relax. Let the thoughts of the day float gently away from your mind. Don't struggle; don't try to push them away. Simply allow them to leave.

Now tense up your toes. Hold them tight for a few seconds. Then release. Feel the tension flowing out of them. Now do the same thing with the feet, then the calves. Tighten. Hold. Release. Let them fully relax. Imagine that someone has yanked a stopper out of your heel and all the tension and tightness of the day is leaking out of you. Gradually do this all through your body—up through the thighs, the buttocks, the abdomen, into the chest, the shoulders, the neck, and the arms. Tighten the muscles. Hold them. Then release. Let them relax, float, tingle. Soon your whole body will seem to float.

Now begin rhythmic breathing. Inhale deeply, all the way into your lungs. Breathe with your abdomen, not the upper chest. Imagine that your abdomen is a balloon. Inhale confidence and strength and energy and fill the balloon. Hold your breath for five seconds. Exhale. Do it again—inhale, hold, exhale. Do this half a dozen times. Now you should feel very relaxed.

Next, close your eyes. It is time to focus sharply, to narrow your thoughts down to one. Concentrate on a single object or idea. Water, perhaps. Let your mind become the placid surface of a pond. Or maybe you are at the ocean in your mind and you can hear the rhythmic ebb and flow of the tide. Or think of a word, the number one perhaps, or your middle name, or the Tibetan word *Om* (meaning that which is behind it all), which is universally used. Repeat the word over and over in your mind. This is known as a mantra and its purpose is to direct your thoughts onto one thing so that all other thoughts will vanish. In time the mantra will also vanish. Stay with the one thought, the one word. Say it over and over. Begin by saying it out loud, then softer, then only in your mind, softer and softer until you are not even certain that you are saying it. Don't try to pound it in. If your thoughts drift, don't try to drag them back to the mantra. Gently prod them. In your mind create a stream that causes them to flow back to the center, the word or thought you are using. After a while you will not need the word. You will be in a peaceful no-mind state. When you are ready to come out of the meditation, stop gradually. Just relax for three to four minutes. Open your eyes slowly. Sit for a minute or two before you move. Allow your energy to return to its normal level. You will find that the more you meditate, the easier it will be.

If you do this daily you will be well on your way to peace. It's not the only way, but it is a way.

INNER PEACE AND THE MARTIAL ARTS

When was the last time someone called you up and proposed a couple of sets of tennis to get a little inner peace? I'll bet it wasn't recently. Nobody seems to talk about inner peace through tennis or inner peace through golf or inner peace through backgammon. But when the subject of martial arts is brought up, most people automatically associate it with the search for inner peace. In fact, for many people, the quest for inner peace is their primary reason for getting involved in the fighting arts. Martial arts are not a hobby that can be isolated from the rest of your life. You take time out to play tennis or basketball, but you don't take time out to "play" at the martial arts. They are always there, and what you know of them pervades all that you do. The physical, mental, and spiritual aspects are inseparable.

29

The martial arts are an appropriate path to inner peace for several reasons. One is that the martial arts are not a competitive sport. Your progress in the arts is marked by the awarding of belts of different colors ranging from white for beginners to degrees of black for the more advanced. It is good to have this recognition that you have mastered certain skills, but that's all it is. The belt is only an acknowledgment, not a goal. The successful martial artist does not go around saying, "Gee, this guy's got a brown belt and I've only got a green one. I better work hard to get ahead of him." The student does not plan and scheme and worry about getting his next colored belt like some businessman trying to close a deal before the end of the month. He doesn't compete. The only person he really wants to be better than is the person he was yesterday. He deals with the present, not the future. I tell all my students, "You're working to earn the belt you're wearing." Inner peace in the martial arts does not come from having done; it comes from doing.

The martial arts bring inner peace for other reasons. There is solitude in the discipline. There is harmony with nature. And there is that immense sense of safety and satisfaction that comes with knowing that if some thug should attempt to assault you on the street, you can annihilate him in less time than it takes you to tie your shoe.

What exactly is inner peace? You could say it's a sort of magic that can be worked through the martial arts. But it's certainly not some supernatural spirit that invades your body only when the time is right. To me inner peace is confidence. And it is living in the now, experiencing each moment as it occurs, not obsessing constantly about past mistakes and future plans. Inner peace is being the eye of the hurricane, peaceful even as turbulent events swirl around you. I think having inner peace means you are controlling your environment; it is not controlling you.

Though I am still growing, I believe I have found inner peace through the martial arts. It is woven into the reality of my everyday life. I tell my students to view inner peace not as an insulation from real life, but as contact with it. To achieve inner peace you don't have to quit your job, abandon your family, and shuffle off in flowing robes to some mountaintop monastery.

At least twice a week I hear from students who want to describe for me the personal growth they have made in the martial arts. It seems as if most have some point at which inner peace came into focus for them. The old anxieties and the insecurities are somehow washed away by the new skills and discipline. One longtime student tells this story:

"When I was in school I was painfully shy. I was afraid to give oral reports in class. My voice was high-pitched to begin with and it would jump another octave when I had to talk in front of people. Then I'd get more nervous and start trembling and sweating."

After this student made the martial arts a part of his life, he noticed big changes in himself. His voice doesn't crack anymore. He's got confidence. He's got inner peace. And he's not afraid to stand up and talk to people. In fact, he's an instructor now in one of my New England schools.

"I think the big change for me came when I got my black belt," he says. "I mean the test for black belt is such a test of the spirit that sometimes I just wanted to die. But when I made it, I knew I could survive anything. That day I felt so proud!"

BE OPEN-MINDED AND FLEXIBLE

It's been said that growth is the knowledge that anything is possible. This also describes open-mindedness. We all have strong opinions, not least of all me, but don't let those opinions block your view of greater knowledge and good new ideas.

As I said before, no one system is the ultimate martial-arts system. Just because you are studying karate, for example, don't assume you can't be taught something by a judo master or even a good middleweight boxer.

And don't assume that because a technique is ancient it must be "the right way." There are many techniques that are five thousand years old but won't work today because they are not applicable to today's real-life situations. There are new concepts, new ideas.

On the other hand, don't assume that something new is automatically better than something ancient. It's not. And if you've been studying the martial arts for three years, or even thirty years, don't assume that the guy who just walked through the *dojo* door can't show you anything. Maybe he can. Maybe he discovered something out on the street. Maybe you can learn it. And if you don't learn it, maybe someday he'll beat you with it.

Always strive for a better way. They build better airplanes every year, better spaceships. They improve everything from TVs to computers. Why not the martial arts? There have been many, many times when I have improved on a weak technique. I never lie to myself. Why should I use a technique that doesn't work? I look at the technique and I say to myself, *Okay, what are the weaknesses? How can it be improved?* I turn the technique around in my mind as if it were a three-dimensional puzzle. I look at it sideways, upside down, inside out. You can improve your technique. But remember, improvement is born and nurtured only in the open mind.

DEVELOP THE MIND

From time to time you will hear someone refer to the martial arts as a psychoscience. That's okay; you won't catch anything from it. It means that the martial arts are a science of the mind as much as anything else.

A continuous development of the mind is essential to success in the martial arts. In fact, probably the greatest benefit you will acquire from the discipline besides physical conditioning and your ability to thrash an attacker will be the mental benefits. As you train your body, you will train your mind. As you strengthen your body, you will strengthen your mind. The mind has unlimited resources. It is the most important tool of the martial artist.

Unfortunately, many systems today don't develop the mind. They develop that five-thousand-year-old punch or stance, but they don't teach their students to think for themselves and develop what is best for them. So when you go looking for a martial-arts program, if you haven't already found one, choose one that puts strong emphasis on development of the mind.

You can grab anybody off the sidewalk and teach him martial-arts skills to a point. But physical skills alone won't take him

By focusing all of your energy into one small area, you create
a tremendous impact that can put your attacker out of action
immediately.

very far. In real life the body reaches limits, but the mind does not. Training will make your body and your mind quicker. However, as you get older, the body will shed some of its quickness no matter how well you take care of it. That's real life. I know I'm a faster and a much more skillful fighter now, at thirty-nine, than I was at twenty-one, because I have always tried to develop my mind. Remember the words of Wang Chung-Yueh: "When an old man is able to defeat many attackers, how could it be due to his strength?"

CONCENTRATION

In the martial arts, as in most endeavors, you should do one thing at a time. In other words, concentrate.

To me, concentration means gathering all of your physical and mental energy into the smallest possible place so that it has maximum impact. The place might be a moment in time, it might be a problem you are trying to solve, or it might be a physical location such as the groin of a would-be rapist. But wherever that place is, be there. Do what you are doing when you are doing it and do nothing else. If you are practicing your breathing, then just breathe. If you are doing a fighting form (*kata*), then just do that. If you are fighting, then just fight. And if you are planning the monthly budget, then just plan the monthly budget. But don't plan the monthly budget while you are doing the *kata,* and certainly not while you are fighting, or you will be planning it from a horizontal position.

The effective martial artist concentrates. He takes each thing as it comes along, finishes it, then goes on to the next. He is not concerned with mistakes of the past or plans for the future. His mind is tight and strong. He knows that a loose mind scatters thoughts and wastes energy.

When you are fighting, your opponent will try to break your concentration. If he's a martial artist, he will probably *kiai* (that's a shout we'll talk more about later). If he's some street punk, he'll probably have something nasty to say about your looks or your heritage. If someone is yelling at you and calling you a swine and threatening to wreck your head, resist the temptation to yell and scream back. The more he yells, the more you should relax, float, concentrate on what you are doing. Don't debate him, just beat him. You can yell at him as much as you want after he's laid out flat on the ground. And one of the reasons he'll be down there is that he broke his own concentration and dispersed his energy with all his moronic shouting.

It is not easy to learn to concentrate. Nobody expects you to arrive at the *dojo* with great powers of concentration. It comes slowly. But it can be developed through practice, discipline, and meditation.

EMPTY YOUR MIND

The world of martial arts is enriched by many stories that are passed from teacher to student to teacher. Most of them involve a Zen master and a student, and they all contain some lesson that can be applied to the martial arts and to life in general.

One of them goes like this:

There was a cocky young street fighter who decided he'd enroll in the new martial-arts studio that had just opened down the street; he figured he'd show them a thing or two. So he went down to the studio to talk it over with the instructor, who was a grand master. The grand master had a kitchenette in the back of his shop and he was making tea, so he invited the street fighter to join him for a cup. The street fighter took a seat and started bragging immediately about how he had beat the tar out of six guys just last week, and how he had already racked up twenty-seven beatings this year. He told the grand master about all these great techniques he had, and how fast he was, and how strong and clever. He said his nickname was, in fact, "fast hands."

When it came time to pour the tea, the grand master filled the young street fighter's cup. When it was full, the grand master kept pouring until the cup overflowed and the tea spilled over the table and onto the young man's lap. The young street fighter leaped to his feet and screamed, "What the hell are you doing? It won't hold anymore."

The grand master smiled. "Like your mind," he said.

"Huh?"

"Your mind is so full of what you think you know that you have left no room for what I can teach you. You must first empty your mind as you would empty this cup. Then we can begin."

The concept of emptying your cup, of forgetting what you have learned, is often useful in the martial arts. Be open to new ideas. Accept the fact that there are things you don't know, and that some of what you do know is best forgotten.

Unless you've been working at the martial arts for many years, you shouldn't have a full cup. But there are probably a few drops of stale tea lingering at the bottom of your cup. Like many things (and even many people), the martial arts have a public image that is often in conflict with reality. If you picked the average guy out of a crowd and asked him what he knew about the martial arts, he'd probably come up with five or six popular images. Most of them would be wrong. Those images are the stale tea I want to wash from your cup as we go along.

ATTITUDE

It's been said that the martial arts are 90 percent mental and 10 percent physical. I might quibble about a percentage point or two, but the message is clear: Attitude is just as important as aptitude. What you think, what you believe, and what you know will determine what you do in the martial arts. It is your mind that guides your behavior.

Attitude is the platform on which you build the knowledge, training, and strength that give you ability. If the platform is weak and soft, if it's made of cheap plywood that cracks at the slightest stress, then what you build on it will never be dependable. A good attitude is a strong platform. Without it you will never capture the true fighting spirit of the martial arts. Without it your martial-arts training will amount to nothing. While it can take months and years for you to get a firm grip on the mental and physical principles we are discussing, a good attitude is something you should bring with you when you walk through the door for your first day of training.

36

CONFIDENCE

By now you've caught on that I rate confidence pretty high on the list of qualities the successful martial artist should have. I guess we all talk a lot about confidence, even though the term is a bit hard to pin down. The first definition of confidence in my dictionary is "trust in a person or thing." The person you should trust in is you. That's confidence. And the thing you should trust in is an observable and predictable pattern. You are confident that the sun will rise tomorrow morning because it always does. You are confident that taxes will also rise, if not tomorrow then next year, because they always do.

Self-confidence, quite simply, is the ability to predict things about yourself in the same dispassionate way that you predict them about other people. When you are confident you do not allow the logic of your conclusions to be tarnished by self-doubt and insecurity. You do not dwell on failures, mistakes, and regrets.

To begin thinking like a confident person, look at the patterns of success in your life. Are you good at something? Were you always good at it? How did you get good at it? Did you ever make mistakes along the way? Of course you did! Did those mistakes prevent you from eventually becoming good at it? No.

To be truly confident is to believe in things you already know. You know that people improve by practicing. You know that if a person sticks to something he becomes faster, stronger, wiser; he becomes better at it. You know that good teachers can pass their knowledge along to you. Being confident doesn't mean you have to be great. It just means you have to believe you can become great. And confidence helps you achieve that greatness, whether it's in the martial arts or in any other field. In many ways, confidence is just common sense. Observe yourself in the same way you would look at anybody trying to learn anything, and draw logical, not emotional, conclusions about what you can accomplish in the martial arts.

Remember this: If you want success in the martial arts, whether you're trying to achieve fighting skills, physical conditioning, weight loss, or inner peace, you must have confidence in yourself.

Self-confidence is the foundation for success at anything. You must believe you are valuable, capable, and competent, and you must be sure of it. You must know that you can leap far beyond the limits that surround you today.

But being confident that you can do something is not the same as pretending that you know all the answers. The confident person knows how to say "I don't know. Please tell me," or "Please show me," or "Please point me toward the information that I need."

I certainly didn't know all the answers about writing a book when I started. I knew the publishing industry about as well as I knew the history of Romanian opera. But I learned. Through it all I never allowed myself to believe I could not do it. I knew that ignorance on any subject is an opponent you can easily take to the mat if you've got confidence and if you are willing to admit that there are things you don't know. If you truly want to, *you can learn anything,* whether it's how to draw or how to dispatch three thugs in seven seconds. You'll make mistakes, but you'll learn from them. So banish any doubts you have about your ability to succeed in the martial arts or anything else. To think about defeat is to take a step toward it.

When I visualize confidence I see it as forward motion. Confidence is not looking back ("Oh, I made a mistake."). Confidence is looking ahead ("What's next?").

Confidence cannot be isolated. Don't strive to be confident in the martial arts. Strive to be confident in life. And remember, the confident person doesn't think about the problem. He thinks about the solution.

PATIENCE

When you begin your martial arts training you should not have the goal of acquiring a colored belt or a certificate to hang on your wall. It's nice to have some tangible proof of your accomplishments, but these things should be results of your efforts, not the reasons for them.

Your goal should be to improve, to grow in the martial arts. You want to become faster, stronger, healthier, calmer, and wiser than you were yesterday. It doesn't matter whether your growth is swift or slow. You'll get there when you get there. There is no final stop on your martial-arts journey, so it is futile to try to reach it faster. You will never reach some ultimate point of good health, speed, or strength. The martial arts are a journey, not a destination, and you will never know all there is to know about them because the arts themselves continue to grow.

So be patient. Move forward at the pace that is best for you. Be proud of your progress, not frustrated about what you don't yet know. Accept the fact that if you're starting out, your muscles may be a bit tight, you may be a bit slow, you may tire easily. If you didn't have something that needed improvement, you wouldn't have begun a program in the first place. Just accept yourself as you are at any given moment and live in that moment. Don't water down the present by thinking constantly about the future.

One way to learn patience is to practice it in small things. If you're anxious to make a phone call, put it off for an hour. If you usually rip open the mail the minute it arrives, try putting it on the shelf for a couple of hours. You'll find that you are learning patience. That also is growth.

THINK POSITIVELY

In the martial arts, as in all of life, almost any event or moment may be viewed in either a negative way or a positive way. The negative view is the most direct path to failure. The positive view leads to success. The negative thinker says, "I got tired after only twenty minutes of exercise today." The positive thinker says, "I went twenty minutes before I got tired. Yesterday it was only fifteen." The negative thinker says, "I made ten mistakes today." The positive thinker says, "I learned ten things today." The negative thinker says, "I got hit hard and it hurt." The positive thinker says, "I got hit hard and that brings me one step closer to eliminating the fear of getting hit."

Practice this. Every time you hear a negative statement coming out of your mouth, follow it with a positive statement about the same information. In time, positive thinking will become your habit.

ELIMINATE FEAR

When a French colonel punished a young officer for showing fear during his first battle, Marshal Foch reprimanded the colonel. "Colonel," he said, "none but a coward dares to boast that he has never known fear."

It's true. We've all been afraid of something—a stranger following us on a dark night, a doctor's diagnosis, or simply speaking in public. Fear is nothing to be ashamed of.

Fear can even be useful. Sometimes it prevents you from entering a dangerous situation. You're afraid of being burned to death so you don't walk into a house that's on fire. In that case, your fear serves you well. But in a situation that is going to exist whether you like it or not, such as your being stalked by a pair of muggers who intend to break your arm and take your wallet, fear has no value. Fear, in a situation like that, is crippling. It slows you down. It fills you with doubt. It corrupts your judgment and wrecks your timing. You cannot live happily with fear, whether it's the fear of losing your job, of getting turned down for a date, or of being whacked over the head by a couple of sickies. To become a superior fighting artist, you must learn to eliminate fear.

Of course eliminating fear is not something you do some rainy afternoon when you're not too busy. It's an attitude, a development of the mind, and it takes time. But it is essential, because if you do not defeat fear, fear will defeat you every time. When you eliminate fear from your life in the martial arts, you will eliminate fear from your life in general.

The things we fear often take on monstrous dimensions in our minds. They loom like great hulking beasts that are preparing to devour us. This gives our fears power over us. Our fears dictate our behavior, or sometimes they nail us in place. We become immobilized.

You can begin to eliminate fear by cutting these frightening ideas down to their proper size. Whenever I put on a martial-arts clinic for two or three hundred students, I pull out the sharpest, shiniest, scariest looking knife that I can find and I grind the blade around in my hand real hard as if I am wringing out a wet face cloth. I just hold it tightly in my bare hand and I twist. If I feared the knife, I would be cut, but by elimi-

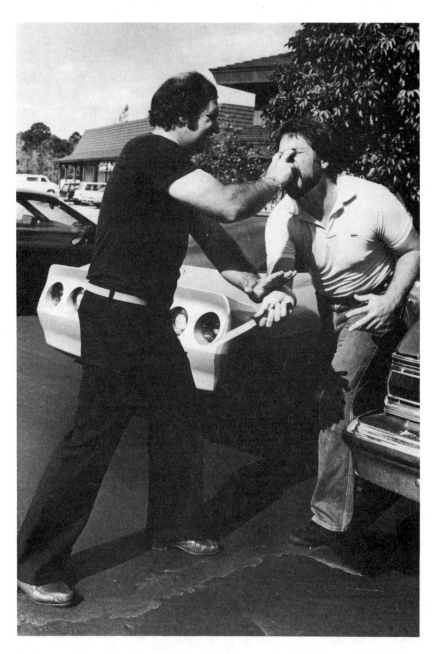

You should respect your attacker's weapon, but not fear it. Try to put it away from the action as quickly as possible.

nating the fear of it I am not. I'm not advising you to do this, and I don't do it myself because I'm anxious to lose a couple of fingers. I do it to make a point. A knife is just a knife. That's all it is. Sure, it looks frightening when someone's waving it at you, but it is just a thing, a helpless object. It has no magical powers. A knife cannot hurt you. Only the individual who's holding the knife can hurt you, and if you know how to show him the error of his ways, you will have no problem.

So get familiar with the knife and all the other weapons that criminals use. See it for what it is—a small, helpless object—and you will not fear it when you see it in the hands of an attacker. You will act against it out of knowledge and logic, not the emotion of fear. The same goes for the attacker's body. It is an object. A big guy might seem frightening until you teach yourself that he's just a man, no more. Sure he's big, but he hurts when you hit him, he bleeds when you cut him, and he makes a tremendous thud when you direct him toward the center of the earth with a felling technique.

Another way to eliminate fear is to confront the things you're afraid of. All of us have postponed dental appointments for weeks because we feared the pain of the drill. Usually, when we finally drag ourselves into the dentist's office, we find that the pain of dentistry is largely a myth, a fear left over from childhood. Confront your fears. Call the girl or guy for a date, get the wart removed, ask for the raise, walk into the dark room.

In the training studio, fear is erased largely through sparring with other fighters. That's what sparring is all about—learning not to fear an attacker.

The most important key to eliminating fear is controlled rhythmic breathing. If a guy pulls out a knife and you believe he's going to cut you, the first thing that happens is you become stiff and tight and your breathing becomes irregular. If you learn to control the breathing, you'll learn to banish fear. Later, I will give you a breathing routine. Proper breathing is essential to all aspects of the martial arts.

Another way to eliminate fear is simply to learn to defend yourself, which is the whole point of martial arts. If you've learned fighting principles and techniques, if you've made yourself faster, stronger, and wiser, you're not going to fear anything because you'll know that twenty-four hours a day you are carrying a deadly weapon. It is you.

Speed, strength, and wisdom are among the weapons in your arsenal, and when you have developed your martial-arts skills, they will always be with you.

ELIMINATE EMOTIONS

Just as you must eliminate fear, you must also eliminate all other emotions from your martial-arts training and fighting. Most people are ruled by emotions and that often leads to failure in business, in relationships, and in athletics. If your decisions are dictated by emotions, your judgment will be blunted and you will fail.

If you attack an opponent out of hate, you will lose. If you try to execute a fancy kick to the temple out of a need for applause, you will lose. If you're determined to win a sparring match because you got fired yesterday afternoon and your ego needs a boost, you will lose. If you strike out of greed (maybe you've bet three hundred dollars on a point sparring match), you will lose.

The effective weapons in any martial artist's arsenal are the things he knows, not the things he feels. By *know,* I don't necessarily mean in the intellectual sense. Your body can know a lot. Your being, your soul, your essence, whatever you want to call it, can know a lot. What you know can often direct your actions without passing through any intellectual process. This is the "no-mind principle" and we'll discuss that next. For now, I just want you to know that a technique that is influenced by emotions is not a reliable technique. Certainly your emotions are important and they have their place, but that place is not in a fight and it is not in the *dojo.*

A workout at the training studio should be an emotional vacation. If you've had a fight with your wife, leave your anger out on the sidewalk. It won't be there when you come out. In the training studio you don't have to fear anyone. You don't have to impress anyone. You don't have to beat anyone. You don't have to prove anything to anyone. You just have to be.

THE NO-MIND PRINCIPLE

In your early martial-arts training you must do a lot of thinking. You've been loaded up with new information and it sits atop your consciousness waiting for you to look it over to see what is useful. It has not had time yet to sink deeply into your unconscious. Even when you begin to spar you will try to think about what you are going to do next. Are you going to punch? Are you going to kick? That's okay, that's how we begin to learn—by considering information in a conscious intellectual way. But after learning comes knowing. And to really know something means not to have to think about it. You must reach the state that the Japanese call *mushin*, which means "no-mind."

Takuan, a great Zen master and swordsman, described it this way:

> The mind must always be in the state of "flowing," for when it stops anywhere that means the flow is interrupted and it is this interruption that is injurious to the well being of the mind. In the case of the swordsman, it means death.
>
> When the swordsman stands against his opponent, he is not to think of the opponent, nor of himself, nor of his enemy's sword movements. He just stands there with his sword which, forgetful of all technique, is ready to follow the dictates of the unconscious. The man has effaced himself as the wielder of the sword. When he strikes, it is not the man but the sword in the hand of the unconscious that strikes.

This state of no-mind, which is achieved through meditation and practice, is not exotic. It is not far removed from daily life. You reach it in a number of activities. Driving a car, for example. When you learned to drive you thought about everything. *Where's the clutch? Where's the brake? What does this funny little switch do?* But now when you drive and you see a red light up ahead you don't think, *Oh, there's a red light. A red light means stop. I'll apply my foot slowly, yet firmly, to the brake pedal, and the brake pedal will cause the car to stop.* You don't think any of these things. You just do them without thinking. That's *mushin*.

When you fight, your mind should flow, not jump. The no-mind principle means you separate the fighter from the fight. Unconscious action is the freest action, the most uninhibited. Let no thoughts interfere with the action. Don't stop to think, just as you don't stop to be afraid or to experience emotions like anger. Toss away the feeling that you are doing it, and just do it. Let your mind and your body float like the dragon that rides on the wind.

When you stop to think or feel, there is an instant of time. It is perhaps only the smallest part of a second, but it is a wasted interval during which your opponent gains an advantage because you cannot respond fast enough to counter his move.

But when your mind floats, when you are without thought, you will see your opponent in slow motion. If you eliminate thoughts, you also get rid of the spaces between the thoughts. It's as if you have twice as much time, so the opponent appears to be moving half as fast. Your observation and your reaction become almost one.

A mind that is empty of thought will not come easily to you. Be patient. You cannot force it. Meditate daily. Practice often. And one day you will be sparring, or perhaps doing a *kata,* and you will look down and see that your arm has moved or your foot has moved and you will say, "How did that get there?" It got there because you knew to put it there without using your conscious mind. In time this will come to you as easily as driving a car. Your responses will become instinctive. But these are not the old instincts; they are the new ones based on what you have learned in your training.

From time to time we all lose the ability to have no thoughts, just as we all have our concentration shattered now and then. It usually happens when emotions seep in. Maybe you've been hit a couple of times recently and you're starting to experience fear again. Or it can happen when you become obsessive about something else in your life. Your kid's flunking math, or your dog has disappeared, or your girlfriend ran off with your best friend. If you lose the *mushin,* don't try to grab it back. Let it come back. Meditate. Relax. Float. It will return.

TREAT ALL OPPONENTS THE SAME

In your mind view all opponents the same way. Certainly there are different ways of fighting different opponents, and we'll discuss them in this book. But in your mind treat all opponents with the same amount of respect. Don't think that just because a guy weighs 100 pounds you can drop him easily. And if a guy weighs in at 310, don't assume he's going to be slow until you've seen his slowness. It doesn't matter whether you are fighting a black belt, a truck driver, a hairdresser, or a drunk on the street. Never let your guard down because an opponent looks like a pushover. Don't evaluate him. Just beat him.

FIGHT TO BEAT YOUR OPPONENT, NOT TO IMPRESS HIM

The essence of fighting is to beat your opponent, not to look pretty.

One of my most vivid childhood memories is of an incident that occurred one morning between my father and two goons. My father was working on a scaffolding, minding his own business, and I was helping him. These two Neanderthals showed up and started hassling him about something or other, and after a few minutes one of these creeps reached into his pocket and pulled out a small knife. In a flash my father leaped down from the scaffolding and decked both of them before he hit the ground. My father knew the principle of beating your opponent and not wasting any time. Whatever he did that day was too fast for anyone to tell whether his form was pretty. It worked, and that's what counts. From that incident I learned an important lesson and, where fighting is concerned, it has made a lasting impression on me.

In fighting, the most effective move is the one that nobody sees. To me, the prettiest punch in western boxing is the one that leaves people asking, "What the hell did he do? Was it an upper cut, was it a hook? What was it?" It was so fast that they didn't see it.

Don't get obsessive about the way you look when you're fighting. Just get the job done.

Over the years I've noticed that many fighting artists, especially tournament fighters, seem most interested in showing off their picture-pretty punch or kick, as if they are being scouted by a movie producer who is anxious to discover the next Bruce Lee. Great form is important, but only to the extent that it makes technique efficient. Form for the sake of form is of no value, and many fighters get so obsessed with appearances that they forget to use effective techniques. Be honest with yourself. U

47

only what works and discard what you find is weak—even if it does look good.

And while we're on the subject of appearances, I'd like to say a thing or two about martial-arts movies. They are great for motivating people. I'm sure many people got turned on to the martial arts after seeing a movie. But a movie theater is not a place of training, and you can't learn the fighting arts by going to kung fu movies every Saturday afternoon. The goal of the movie is to entertain, so the fighters are not necessarily using techniques that work. They are using techniques that look good up there on the silver screen. So you see a lot of guys leaping over buildings and cars and a lot of moves that look more like acrobatic routines from the circus than fighting techniques appropriate for today's real-life situations.

USE YOUR STRENGTHS

Gwenn is a woman who often works out in my studio headquarters in Massachusetts. She is about thirty-five years old and in good shape now, though she wasn't when she first signed up. I used to watch Gwenn practice and it seemed to me that she was spending half her time trying to develop a high kick with her right leg. The kick would get just so high, then Gwenn would wince and drop it. Then she'd take a deep breath and try again. Two or three times a week I'd see her going through the fighting forms known as *katas*. She was coming along well, but she was spending much too much time on that high kick.

Finally, I went over to her one day when she was struggling to get that leg up higher.

"What's the matter?" I asked.

"The kick," she said.

"What about it?"

"I can't do it," she said. She sounded frustrated. "I can't get it higher." She told me she'd had an operation on that leg and it just wouldn't rise above her waist.

"So," I said. "Why do you want to get it higher?"

"Well you have to, don't you?" she asked.

"No," I said. "You just have to do what works. You're fast, you've got excellent balance. Use that."

"Huh?"

48

"Look at it this way," I said. "You're strong for your size, but no matter what you do you are never going to be as strong as the deranged six-foot rapist who follows you down a dark street. But it's okay, you don't have to be. You'll defeat him in some other way. You're not going to overpower a big man, but you're still going to beat him. By the same token, maybe fate has decided that you are never going to kick him in the ribs either because your foot is never going to go high enough. But that's okay. Go with what works, not what doesn't."

I was telling Gwenn to use her strengths. We're all different. Some of us are slow, but big. Some of us have a lightning fast punch, but a kick that looks as if it stopped for dinner along the way. Some of us can't hit hard, but we move like panthers. You should develop fighting techniques that utilize your strengths and minimize your weaknesses. There is an infinite number of fighting styles. You might as well use one that's designed for you. When I get a student who's been studying for a while, yet doesn't have a very strong kick, I don't spend years trying to make him a strong kicker. I develop the holding, hitting, and felling aspects of his technique. I emphasize his strengths, not his weaknesses. Do this in the martial arts, and do this in real life.

So, how do you know your strengths? You don't. Not until you get into the training studio and work with a good teacher. The new martial artist is rarely the best judge of his own strengths and weaknesses.

About six years ago a guy came into my studio and wanted to sign up for a program. While I gave him a tour of the facilities, he kept assuring me over and over that his legs would be practically useless to him. "The knees are bad," he kept saying. "The knees are bad. They creak when I just go for a walk."

This guy's main problem was that he wasn't exercising properly or regularly. The knees *were* bad. But they weren't terminal. The man, quite simply, was out of shape. After he worked out for a bit, slowly at first, he got his knees back to normal. Then he got them better than normal. They were loose, strong; they never hurt. From there, he worked more and more on his kicks. I see him in the studio now and then. Today he is the proud holder of a black belt, and he's a fine kicking technician, with fast, powerful hands.

So as you grow in the martial arts, emphasize your strengths.

49

But don't make assumptions about what those strengths are until you've worked thoroughly on everything. You may have more strengths than you think. Only time, learning, and practice will tell you.

USE YOUR OPPONENT

In real life when you fight, you must take into account all that is true. For example, you must consider the environment. If you are trapped in an elevator with two bloodthirsty thugs, then perhaps you'd better save that flying kick for another day. If you're wearing heavy boots, use hand strikes and forget about the fancy footwork that dazzled them down at the training studio.

But by far the most significant element for you to consider in a real-life fight is the opponent. He is real. He has strength. He has size. He has, possibly, a degree of insanity. And you cannot change any of that by making special rules. In a real fight there are no rules. So just as you must learn to use your own strengths and minimize your weaknesses, you must learn to maximize your opponents' weaknesses and use his strengths, or at least neutralize them. You cannot assume anything about him. You must learn to read the information quickly. So use the martial artist's greatest weapon, the brain.

If you study at a good martial-arts school, you will learn a lot about using your opponent. For example, if the attacker is bigger than you, he's probably not going to move as fast, and when he does move, he'll be putting more weight in motion. It will take him longer to get back on track and turn to come at you again, just as it takes longer to stop a truck than, say, a Volkswagen. With a person like that, you'd want to work to his side and rear because your advantage is that you can move from side to side faster.

If the attacker is much lighter than you, he could be trickier. The counter is to work him with linear moves. Use strength and forward motion. You employ linear techniques because if you try to work him from the side, he might not be there when you arrive.

If your attacker is particularly fast, you should concentrate on holding and trapping techniques. He can't be so fast that he can beat a trap, since you only have to move your hands a few inches to trap him.

In your martial-arts training, imagine different types of opponents and practice techniques that will neutralize their strengths. For every technique there is a counter, and for every counter there is another counter. And remember, the race does not always go to the swift or to the strong. It usually goes to the smartest and the quickest. In executing fighting techniques, speed and balance are more important than strength. If you have speed and balance, you will become stronger. But if you have strength, that will not necessarily give you speed and balance.

III

PHYSICAL PRINCIPLES

FLOW

There is a book called *Make Every Word Count* (Writer's Digest Books) by Gary Provost. Something Provost said in that book about writing applies equally to the martial arts and is worth repeating.

Provost wrote, "To teach writing one must first make some arbitrary distinctions. A piece of writing is not like a car, for example, where something is either a carburetor or a spark plug no matter how you hold it or where you view it from. You can't unscrew and yank out one part of writing and drop it in a bag without dragging along chunks of all the other parts, but for the purposes of teaching, we pretend that you can do just that.

"If I wanted to teach you how to make a car, it would not be enough just to march you down to your local Ford dealer and have you stare through the showroom window at the new red Mustang. I'd have to throw open the hood, rip off the doors, thresh out every screw and wire in that car, and lay the parts across the floor. Then I would have to piece them all back together again so that you could see how the car was made. In fact I would have to do this several times for you to understand.

"So to teach you to write, I'll have to pretend that writing is like a car as I break it down into parts called 'description,' or 'dialogue,' or 'style.' "

And so it is with the martial arts. In this section I will talk about "parts" of the arts, such as blocking, kicking, and punching. But, in fact, you cannot really isolate them, except for the purpose of discussion. Fighting technique does not jump; it flows. To try to separate one movement from the fight would be like trying to separate the water from the river. No motion is wasted in the martial arts. A successful block flows into a successful offensive technique. However, that is a principle of motion and the mind. To get it into words I must, like Provost, pretend that the martial arts are more like a car.

THE *KIAI*

The *kiai* (pronounced key-eye) is a shout used during a fight. It is a psychological weapon which, if not overused, can boost your fighting spirit and frighten your opponent. The *kiai* is used to startle your opponent, to freeze his motion, to shatter his concentration so you can make a move. The *kiai* also maximizes body strength through the expulsion of air and energy.

However, the *kiai* is being improperly used in many styles of fighting. A lot of instructors tell their students to *kiai* on every kick and punch. That is wrong. Every time you *kiai* you expend a lot of energy. You tire sooner. You lose strength and your endurance drops. You could easily lose a fight because you have spent all your energy using the *kiai* after every kick and punch. Use it only on major blows and strikes. Maybe once every ten blows. During practice use it only on every twentieth strike or so.

When you are fighting more than one opponent, it is especially important to save your energy. You need endurance to dispatch multiple opponents effectively, so use the *kiai* properly. If I put two guys side by side and have one *kiai* on every strike and the other *kiai* once out of twenty strikes, the guy who *kiais* less is going to be strong after the shouter has worn himself out.

Try this experiment. Throw kicks and punches and *kiai* on every move for five minutes. How do you feel? Now take another five minutes and throw punches and kicks, but only *kiai* on every twentieth strike. Now how do you feel? Remember, the *kiai* is not free; it costs you some energy.

The most crucial time to use the *kiai* is when you are about to finish off your opponent. After you have hit your man a few times, or kicked him or broken his balance, and have put him into a position where you can end the fight, that is the time to call upon your energy and *kiai*.

The *kiai* maximizes body strength through the expulsion of air and energy

BREATHING

If you don't master breath control, you'll lose. It's that simple. Proper breathing exercises will help you increase your supply of fighting energy. With proper breathing technique a martial artist can spend wisely the energy he has, channel it to a particular point in his body, and direct it for a specific attack or counterattack. Proper breathing makes you the master. You can think more clearly, react more quickly, and strike more effectively. Your lungs become reservoirs of air and strength. Proper breathing is as important to the martial artist as water is to the swimmer.

Try this: Block your nose slightly so that you cannot inhale as much air as you normally do. Not very comfortable, is it? That's how you would feel if you were trapped in an elevator for three hours with six other people. You feel as if you are suffocating. Because you are. Now imagine trying to punch, kick, or jump while you feel that way.

What if I told you that you are already blocking your nose like that all day long? You are. At least you are compared to any martial artist who has learned proper breathing technique. The breathing of most people is shallow. They use only the top half of their lungs, and feed far too little oxygen into the bloodstream. It's like running an eight-cylinder car on only four cylinders. If you don't use all of your breathing capacity, your potential power will never be realized.

The time to start breathing properly is now.

BREATHING EXERCISE

Inhale through the nose deeply, so that you feel it all the way down to your abdomen. Imagine that balloon inside your abdomen. Place your fingers on your abdomen and feel it expand as you inhale. Get the air deep into your lungs. It might help if you visualize the air as a soft, blue mist and suck it right out of the room. Exhale through the mouth. Inhale again. Bring in confidence, strength, and energy to fill the balloon. Exhale fear and insecurity. Inhale. Exhale.

This type of breathing, deep and rhythmic, uses the lungs

58

The effective fighter is the one who maintains his own balance while breaking or disturbing the balance of his opponents.

more effectively. It stimulates the internal organs, it invigorates the whole body. It makes you stronger, happier, more alert. Practice this breathing technique for fifteen minutes every day until proper breathing comes naturally to you.

And remember: Proper breathing is the key to knocking fear out of your life, whether it's the fear of a criminal with a switchblade or of an IRS man with an audit. Before you confront any tense situation, do this breathing exercise for a few minutes. Soon you will be in control. You will be calm. You will be ready to face anything.

BALANCE

I'm tempted to make some bold, broad statement here, such as BALANCE IS EVERYTHING, FOLKS! But I won't. Nothing is everything. But that gives you some idea of how important balance is. It is an essential element in fighting. The effective fighter is the one who maintains his own balance while breaking or disturbing the balance of his opponent. The martial artist guards his balance as vigilantly as he guards his vital areas. When he is fighting, balance is his most precious possession; he must protect it from the intrusion of opponents and from his own mistakes. His balance gives him control. When he loses it he is in danger.

You cannot learn balance from a book. You learn it through practice. In your martial-arts program you learn that your balance can be "weak to the front" if your weight is on the toes of both feet. When your balance is weak to the front, you can easily be pulled forward and introduced to the floor. If your balance is "weak to the back," with your weight on both heels, an attacker can get behind you and pull you down without difficulty, or he can stand in front of you and tip you over like a giant domino. The weakest balance position of all would be to have all your weight on one foot. Then you are an easy target from any direction.

The martial arts are often called the yielding arts. That's because the martial artist does not fight natural forces. He yields to them, he uses them, and the loss of balance often creates those natural forces which the wise martial artist uses.

To understand the principle of balance in a fight you don't have to be a martial artist and you don't have to be in a *dojo*. Without any training at all you could use the principle of balance in real life, tonight. Here's an example:

Let's say you and your wife go into town to a movie, and after the movie some nitwit who's consumed too much alcohol starts harassing you. Let's say he's angry with you because you look like a guy he knew in high school, and he starts calling you names. So you tell him to take a hike, but unfortunately he doesn't feel like taking a hike. Let's also say that he's bigger than you and stronger than you and he decides it would be fun to push you around. The first thing he's going to do is push you at chest level, hoping to provoke you. Let him push. Stand firm. Don't move forward or back. Now he feels the resistance, so you know that next time he's going to push harder. When he pushes harder, don't fight it. He's controlling the direction of the action, so you should go with his flow. Take a step back away from him. Now you still have your balance, but he doesn't. He's just pushed hard and forward and his balance is weak to the front. At this point you simply reach out and take his arm or his collar and yank him forward. All the forces of physics are in your favor and gravity will help you put him face down on the sidewalk. If you happen to be a martial-arts expert, you can now stick around for a little excitement. If you're not, it might be a good time to leave. That's a simple example of using balance, not power, to get the job done. Many martial-arts techniques are built on this principle.

MOMENTUM

In physics, momentum is the product of the mass of a moving particle and its linear velocity. I understand physics about as well as I understand Latvian. But I do know that in real life, momentum means that a moving object, such as a human body for example, prefers to keep moving in the direction it is headed. So it takes a lot less energy to help it than to stop it.

You can quickly demonstrate this principle by placing a quarter on the back of your right hand. Extend your arm out from your right shoulder. Now extend your left arm straight in front of you. Swing your right arm around now so that it will come to a stop when it crashes into the left arm. Watch what happens to the quarter. It continues to go forward. It wants to move in the direction it was going.

In the martial arts, momentum counts for quite a lot. If you are fighting someone and he's coming at you full force, it is better to get out of the way than to try to interrupt that force. Better still, you should go with his flow, use his momentum against him the way you did the drunk who thought you were his high-school enemy. If a man's foot is hell-bent on getting to the space that is occupied by your face, and you leave your face there, his foot will try to continue its direction right through your face and the result will be ugly. You should get out of the way, let the foot go where it wants to go. You know that his foot will continue forward, and the man's body must follow, and his force can become part of your strength if you direct your techniques into the line of that force. Why swim upstream when you can float downstream!

The principle of momentum is present in all martial-arts techniques. Use it often.

VISUALIZATION

One day I was explaining the technique of visualization to a man who had recently begun his martial-arts training when he stopped me and said, "You know, I never thought of it before, but that's how I learned to play basketball."

When he was a kid, he told me, he idolized Bob Cousy of the Boston Celtics. "I used to pretend I was Cousy," he said. "I'd try to walk like the Cooz, dribble like him, throw behind-the-back passes like him, and shoot outside set shots like him. I'd visualize his motion when I played. After a while I got to be a pretty good basketball player and I could throw a behind-the-back pass with the best of them."

That's visualization.

Did you ever imagine that you were in a fight with someone and actually feel your arm jump or your fist leap forward? That's visualization.

Visualization works because the brain does not make a great

distinction between what you do and what you imagine you do. For example, if you think about jogging and really visualize it, the muscles in your legs will contract just as if you were jogging.

I call the technique of visualization going to the movies on the back of your eyelids. But you don't have to close your eyes to visualize. In fact, if you are being stalked down an alley by three enraged members of the Hell's Angels, it would be best not to close your eyes while you visualize the techniques you are going to use to greet them.

Visualization is used in all sports, though the term is rarely used. In golf, for example, as in many other sports, the follow-through is essential for a good swing. At first glance this doesn't seem to make any sense. How can what happens to the swing after contact is made with the ball possibly have any effect on the ball? It doesn't make sense until you view the entire swing as an entity, an entity that existed in mental-picture form before the swing occurred. It is that mental picture which programs the brain and feeds it all the information it needs about speed, power, distance, angle, and balance. If the golfer does not follow through properly, it's because he did not program properly, he did not accurately visualize what he had to do, and that is why his ball is lodged in six inches of mud at the bottom of a pond.

In the martial arts you use visualization in several ways. Most commonly you use it by visualizing a goal that is greater than the real goal. Just as the runner might work out with weights strapped to his ankles to create greater resistance than he will actually have to deal with, the martial artist creates a greater degree of difficulty in his mind. For example, some day you might have to smash a mugger's face. You will get maximum power into that punch if you visualize not that you are punching his face, but that you are punching *through his face*. Visualize your fist going right through. The Chinese call this punching for a thousand miles. Your punch probably won't go quite that far, but it will be a lot more powerful because that's what you aimed for. This is the technique used in demonstrations of board-breaking and brick-breaking. The martial artists don't simply try to hit the board; they try to go through it for a thousand miles.

Here's a visualization exercise you can try. It's called the unbendable arm. Get a partner. Face him. Extend one arm over his shoulder and ask him to try to bend it. If he's of average or superior strength, he'll probably be able to. Now put the arm out again. This time visualize. Imagine that your arm is one of those heavy-duty water hoses that the fire department uses. The hose is engorged with water surging through it at extremely high pressure, and it extends far beyond your partner's shoulder. Way off in the distance you can see the water pouring out of it. Look far beyond your partner and ask him to bend your arm. He won't be able to.

Another experiment: The next time you go for a walk imagine that somebody has put a harness around your waist and is pulling you along with a cable. Visualize it. You will feel your steps quicken. You will feel lighter and swifter and, in fact, you will move faster.

You can use visualization in another way. You can visualize self-defense situations that might come up. Imagine that you see an attacker or attackers. Where are they? What weapons do they have? What techniques, if any, will they try to use on you? Then visualize yourself reacting to this situation, defeating them through proper technique. When the situation does occur, you'll be ready to react correctly.

I don't advise you to use visualization during a real fight until you've done it so much that it comes naturally and you can use it in combination with the no-mind principle. By that I mean that if you have to *think* about what you're going to visualize, you're not ready to use it in a real fight. It is more important to have a clear, uncluttered mind when you are in a fight.

However, with practice, visualization will come to you as easily as breathing, and you will use it in a real fight. For example, you might envision your opponent's arms as the limbs of a tree and you can chop them off with your knife-hand blow. Another way is to visualize yourself as one of the five animals that we will talk about later.

IV

FIGHTING TECHNIQUES

THE FOUR WAYS OF FIGHTING

In my American Shaolin kempo system, there are four ways of fighting. You should use them all. If you emphasize only one or two ways of fighting, you will show your opponent your areas of weakness and the limited extent of your fighting knowledge.

Most systems fully utilize only one or two ways of fighting. I believe in using whatever works, and that includes techniques from all four ways. The way I figure it, if you only know two ways of fighting, you're going to be in serious trouble when you meet a guy who knows three. A lot of instructors are living in some kind of magical fairyland where every guy you fight has been trained in the same system as you. In real life it's not like that. When was the last time you heard a mugger ask his victim what system he was trained in?

The four ways of fighting are hitting, kicking, felling, and holding.

Hitting

Hitting is using any kind of a hand strike: a punch, a closed fist, an open hand. If you strike with the forearm, the wrist, or the shoulder, or jab with the fingers, that also is hitting. Western boxing is a good example of a martial art that uses only hitting. Hitting techniques are generally used from the groin up. The hand, especially, is quick, accurate, and can be used at close range.

Kicking

Kicking refers to any blow you deliver with the feet, the legs, the inner thigh, the knee, the heel—anything below the waist. Kicks are more effective and quicker if your target is the lower part of the body, from the stomach down. Also, kicking to those

HITTING

KICKING

FELLING

HOLDING

areas does not lessen your balance. However, it is good to practice kicking higher for conditioning and strength.

Felling

The felling techniques are the ones that most people associate with judo or jujitsu. To fell something means to knock it down, and a felling technique is any technique you use to put your man on the ground. If you throw a man, trip him, push him, shove him, or sweep him, that's a felling technique. Felling techniques are the ones that most obviously utilize the physical principles of balance, momentum, and leverage.

Holding

Holding techniques, also called grappling techniques, are found in wrestling and aikido. Once you've held and trapped your man in a good holding position, you can go to work on him. Break his bones, break his neck, break his finger, whichever you prefer. Whatever it is, it will certainly break his spirit. The Tiger Claw (page 91) is an example of holding technique.

As you can see, the martial artist who just knows how to kick or punch is going to be a marshmallow for the guy who can hit him, kick him, trap him in a hold, then drop him to the floor and go to work on him. So if you are really serious about becoming a skillful and superior fighter, you must learn all four ways. Western boxing consists of just hitting, aikido—holding, judo—felling, and tae kwon do—kicking. However, my method of American Shaolin kempo consists of all four of these ways of fighting. All methods of fighting, in fact, come from the ancient Chinese Shaolin system.

VITAL TARGETS AND THE POISON HAND

In your martial arts training you will learn that all these techniques are more effective in some spots than in others. The advanced martial artist learns to administer defeat through specific pressure points throughout the body, just as acupuncture practitioners have traditionally learned for healing. These advanced techniques are generally incorporated in the four ways of fighting. They are called poison-hand techniques.

Poison Hand: Poke at the attacker's eyes. If he can't see you he can't hit you.

However, for the beginning or intermediate student who wants to know what to do in a street brawl, some less sophisticated advice about vital points is in order. Do this: Poke at the attacker's eyes; if he can't see you, he can't hit you. Kick to the shin; you know how lovely that feels. Punch to the groin, kick to the groin; that is certainly a vital spot. Thrust the palm upward to the nose. That will surely discourage rapists. Any severe blow to the collarbone will also work wonders. The collarbone is surprisingly easy to break. Also, clap the ears with both hands and/or smash a foot down on the instep. All of these will make your attacker consider the possibility that he has made a mistake.

In your training you will focus on these vital spots, and you will learn techniques that cause your opponent to open up these targets to you.

BLOCKING, DODGING, AND SLIDING

Blocking, dodging, and sliding techniques are very important moves. They can be classified as "the art of not getting hit" because they teach you how to avoid or steer clear of receiving a blow. All the offensive techniques in the world are useless if you are lying on the floor because you couldn't block, dodge, or slide effectively.

But, ideally, blocking, dodging, and sliding do not simply spare you some difficulty. They create a favorable situation for your technique: They set you up for an attack.

There are two blocking systems: hard blocking and soft blocking. The hard block is aggressive and unyielding. You try to stop a blow with the strength of your hand, arm, leg, or body. Hard blocking means you spend a lot of energy, use a lot of force; it can result in injury for the blocker as well as the blockee. Hard blocking is very basic and is considered crude in the martial arts.

The soft-blocking system is a little more consistent with the overall message of the martial arts: Yield to win, use the opponent, go with the flow. The soft block often uses the attacker's forward motion to deflect the attack and break the attacker's balance. The attacker who lunges at you has committed himself. The soft block you use creates an entry point for your own offensive technique, and because you've used a soft block you've conserved your energy to execute that technique.

When you use hard-blocking techniques, be sure to to use them quickly. If an opponent is trying to strike you, the greater the distance his arm or foot has traveled, the more power it will have. If his entire body is coming at you, the momentum is tremendous, and you should really use a soft blocking technique to deflect him in the direction you can best use to your advantage. Your training in blocking, dodging, weaving, and sliding will include a lot of drills, and will emphasize speed and eye-training so that you can get to your target before he gets to you.

V

THE FIVE ANIMALS

BE AN ANIMAL

Did you ever meet a cat who was ashamed of himself because he had failed to catch a mouse? Of course not. The cat doesn't waste time on feeling ashamed, guilty, or apologetic. He just keeps chasing mice, and he learns to react faster, move more quickly, and waste no motion. That's because he's an animal and he hasn't been taught about failure, self-doubt, and lack of confidence. The cat never has an identity crisis, he never goes to therapy, and he never says to Mrs. Cat, "Gee, honey, I don't think I'm cut out for this mouse-chasing stuff."

This is how you should be in the martial arts—like an animal. When we praise a person's physical abilities we often compare him to an animal. We say he's strong as a bull, free as a bird, runs like a cheetah, or has the eyes of a hawk.

An animal uses all of his motion to accomplish his goal, to get the job done. He never tries to impress anybody. He just does what works. I think a tiger in the jungle would probably be the perfect martial-arts student, though it would be hell trying to get him into the *gi* (martial-arts uniform). And among human beings, the best students are the ones who are most able to be like animals.

THE FIVE ANIMALS

Some of the greatest karate teachers have not been people. They've been animals. Martial artists have always learned from the animals, and the movements of a great variety of creatures have found their way into various forms of self-defense.

The ancient masters who developed much of what we use today often studied animals in battle. How did the animal move?

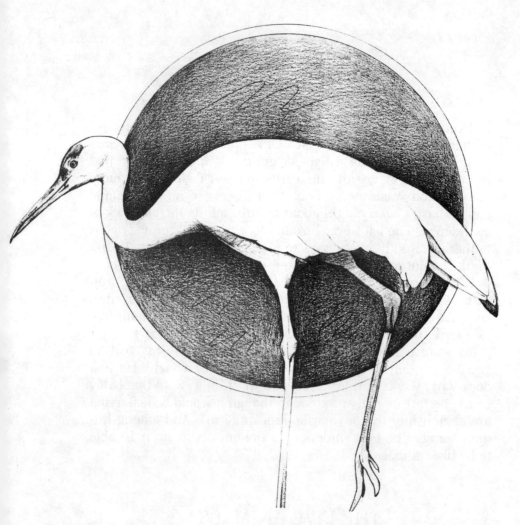

THE CRANE

The crane is like water. It is agile and yielding. It allows the opponent to defeat himself through his own momentum. The crane has excellent balance and is very good at disturbing the balance of others. It has strong wings (arms) and uses them often and effectively.

Crane Strike

To form the Crane Strike:

1. Open your palm wide.
2. Bring the tips of your fingers and thumb to meet at one point which forms the beak.
3. Now bend your wrist, pointing the beak downward.

The Crane Strike is used for poking vital areas, blocking, and striking.

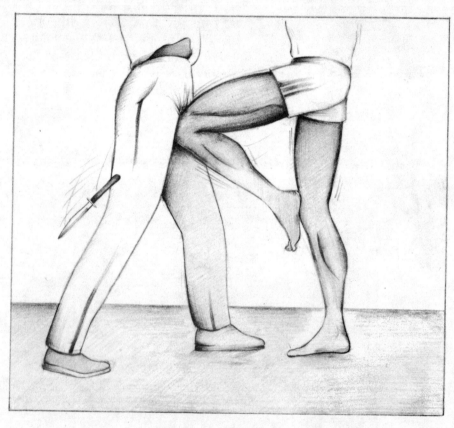

Crane Kick

The knee is used in close to an opponent. This strike may be used in an upward motion, such as to strike the groin. Or it may be used in a circular, "roundhouse," motion to areas such as the side of the leg, the kidneys, the ribs, or the solar plexus, and, with manipulation of the hair or ears, to the head.

Because you are so close to your opponent, this strike uses much of your weight and is therefore powerful.

Upward Knee

1. Start from a forward stance.
2. Bring knee straight up from the ground and out to your target.

Roundhouse Knee

1. Start from a forward stance.
2. Bring your knee out to the side.
3. Move in a circular motion toward your opponent.

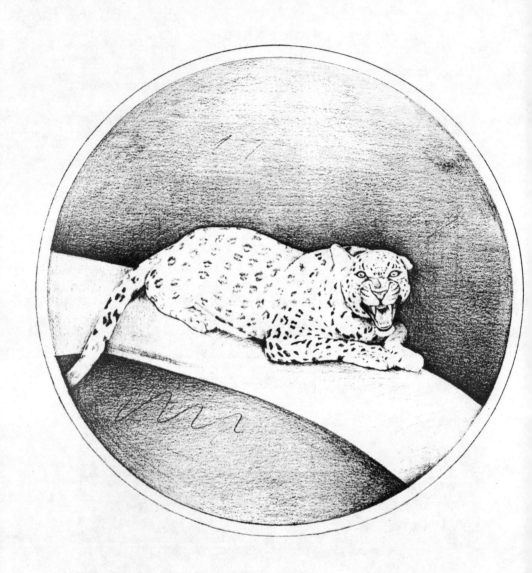

THE LEOPARD

The leopard is mighty. It is faster and more agile than a tiger, but not as powerful. It packs a lot of strength into its frame and has enormous impact. The leopard employs many crushing techniques and a lot of internal strikes with the hands. It is strong and muscular and gets in close to do its damage.

Leopard Paw

To form a Leopard Paw:

1. Open your palm wide.
2. Tuck your thumb in.
3. Keep all your fingers close together.
4. Bend all your fingers at the second joint.

This strike is used in thrusting and punching. It is excellent for breaking ribs and bones.

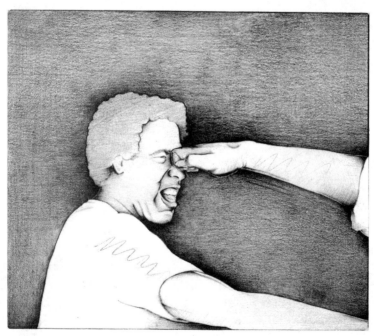

Using the Leopard Paw

85

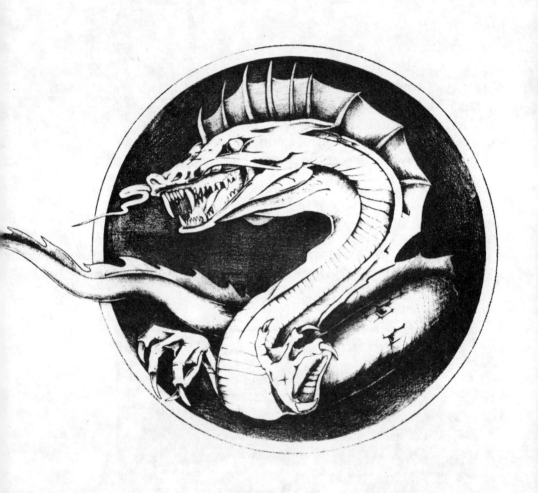

THE DRAGON

The dragon is loose. It has a lot of floating motion and a lot of
swinging around and whipping. It has a powerful tail that has
its analogy in kicking techniques. The dragon's movements develop concentration and will. It is elusive, hard to spot; it uses
many combinations and it's quick. The dragon has an indomi-
table spirit; you cannot destroy one. The dragon is also the
symbol of heaven in Shaolin.

Twin Dragons

To form the Twin Dragons:

1. Open your palm wide.
2. Tuck your thumb in.
3. Bend your last two fingers and tuck them into the palm.
4. Slightly bend your index and middle fingers; spread them wide apart.

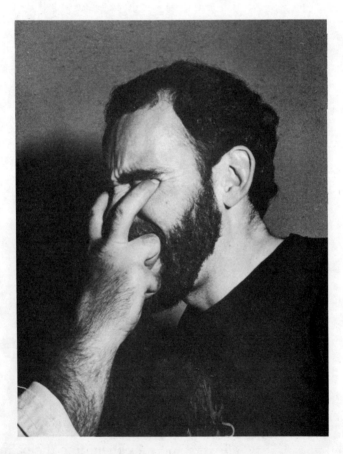

The Twin Dragons is used for poking and thrusting at vital areas. Here, Twin Dragons strike to the eyes.

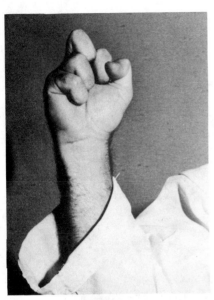

Dragon's Head

To form a Dragon's Head:

1. Start with your palm open.
2. Bend all fingers at the second joint.
3. Bend all but your middle finger at the third joint.
4. Place your thumb over your fingers and clench.

Using the Dragon's Head

THE TIGER

The tiger has ferocity. The Chinese say, "Never disturb a sleeping tiger," and that is sage advice. In the martial arts, the tiger has strength and speed. Its hand strikes are quick and deadly, and its clawing techniques are enough to send any street thug home to Mama.

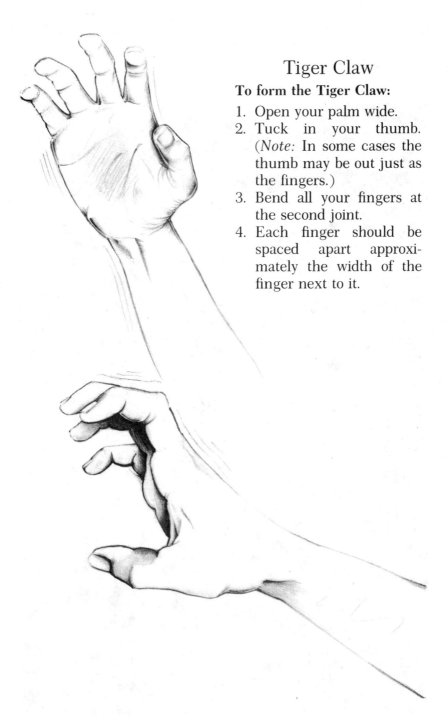

Tiger Claw

To form the Tiger Claw:

1. Open your palm wide.
2. Tuck in your thumb. (*Note:* In some cases the thumb may be out just as the fingers.)
3. Bend all your fingers at the second joint.
4. Each finger should be spaced apart approximately the width of the finger next to it.

The Tiger Claw is used for ripping, gouging, raking, clamping, pulling, thrusting, and holding muscles and vessels.

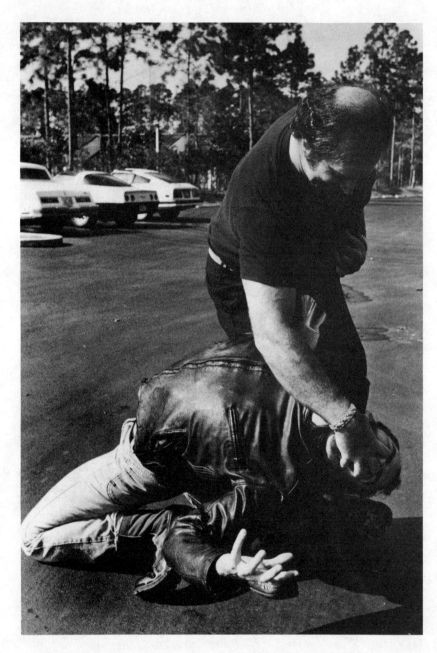

Using the Tiger Claw

THE SNAKE

The snake is powerful and flexible. It is supple and crackles with inner energy. The snake is not so much for holding and, as you might imagine, is not real big on kicking. It goes for the vital points, attacking the ears, the eyes, the throat. The snake uses a lot of choking and restricting techniques. It does a lot of grappling and wrapping around an attacker's body to break and crush things. The snake goes for the pressure points.

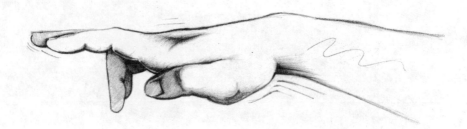

Snake's Head

To form the Snake's Head:

1. Have your palm open wide.
2. Tuck your thumb in.
3. Have your fingers close together and slightly bent.
4. Bend the last two fingers close to the palm.

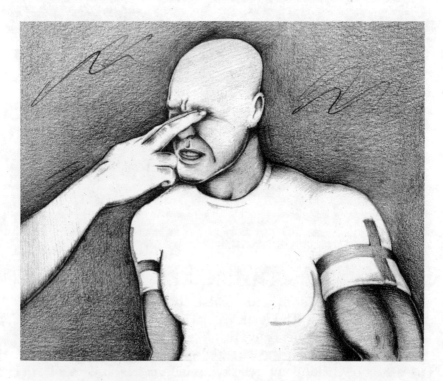

The Snake's Head strike is used for poking and thrusting at vital areas such as the eyes or throat.

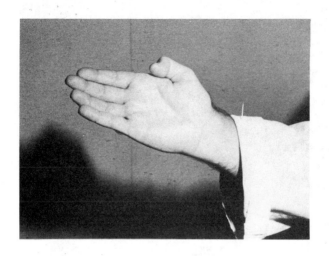

Snake Strike

The formation of the Snake Strike is the same as for the Snake's Head, but you must keep all four fingers together.

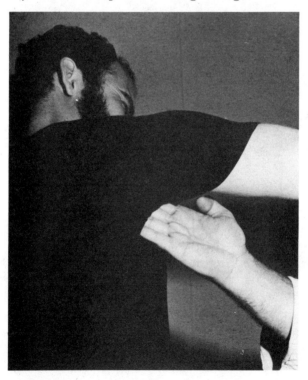

The Snake Strike is used for thrusting and poking and may also be used for penetrating the body to strike at internal organs.

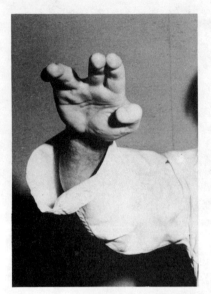

Snake's Tooth

To form the Snake's Tooth:

1. Start with the same hand formation as for the Snake Strike.
2. Separate the middle finger and the ring finger to create an opening between them.

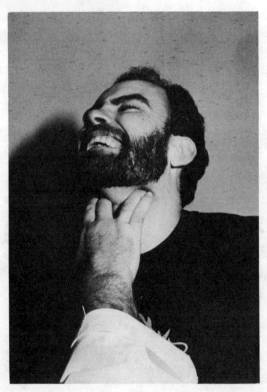

The Snake's Tooth strike is used for poking to areas such as the throat or eyes.

How did he defend himself? How did he adjust to a changing situation? The masters watched. This required the humility of believing they could learn. And from the animals they borrowed whichever moves were appropriate to human bodies and human situations.

Not only do we get many specific moves from the animal kingdom, but we also find there many of the psychological ideas of the martial arts. Take, for example, the idea of using your strengths, which we'll talk more about soon. The cat usually goes into battle against an opponent that is bigger and stronger. Does the cat try to overpower him? No. Does the cat say, "Maybe if I hand over my wallet he'll leave me alone?" No. The cat says, "What is my strength?" and the answer comes back, "Those sharp claws." So the cat aims those sharp claws straight for the eyes of the opponent. In physical terms this shows up as an open-hand slash to the eyes in the art of self-defense, but in philosophical terms it shows us that the cat uses his strengths.

In my system of American Shaolin kempo, we use the movements of five animals: the crane, the leopard, the dragon, the tiger, and the snake. These five animals were used in the days of the ancient Shaolin monastery. I don't want to tell you that these are the five true animals or any such nonsense. Many systems use the bear, the praying mantis, the monkey, even the deer. But these five have worked for me. They are effective, and that's what counts.

It would take an entire book to discuss the movements of these animals, and it will take you years to master them. But briefly I want to give you an idea of how the movements of the animals fit into the overall technique.

As you can see from these examples, each of the animals is associated with certain kinds of motion, movements which they use efficiently and effectively. All of these animals will come into your martial-arts training, and much of your training will center around one animal at a time. For example, iron balls are often used to develop the hand coordination and finger strength that is associated with the tiger. However, when you are fighting, you are not stuck with one type of animal. The martial arts are continuous flowing combinations of animal movements and other techniques.

VI

TRAINING

FINDING A SCHOOL

If you have not already begun your martial-arts training, you might now want to start looking around for a *dojo*. That *dojo* might be a garage, or it might be a plushly carpeted studio. Whatever it is, you should choose carefully and you should choose more on the basis of instruction than environment, though environment is certainly important.

Unfortunately, there is no universal code of quality for martial-arts schools. Any bozo can call himself a martial-arts instructor, hang out a shingle that says KARATE EXPERT, and open a shop. So there's a broad range of instruction available, and not all of it is good. However, if you choose carefully and allow no one to browbeat you, you can find a good martial-arts school almost anywhere in the world.

When you go to look at a martial-arts school, the first thing you should do is check to see if the paint on the door is dry. Many schools vanish into thin air as soon as the second month's rent comes due, either because somebody planned it that way, or because the school didn't attract enough students to make a go of it. I don't mean to imply that a new school can't be good; every school was new at one time. But if the school you're considering hasn't been established for at least a couple of years, give it a little extra scrutiny.

Visit a variety of schools. Any reputable martial-arts school will allow you to come in and observe a few classes without charge. Watch the teacher. He could be a good martial artist but a terrible teacher. How does he handle the students? Does his own ego get in the way of showing what will work best for them?

The instructor should be willing to answer all of your questions. Listen to his pitch. If he's trying too hard to impress you, it might be time to move on to the next school. The true martial-arts teacher is not primarily concerned with hustling up new business, twisting arms, or snatching students off the sidewalk. Obviously, the instructor is trying to make a living. But he can do that best by being a good teacher and acquiring a good reputation. He tells the student what the program can or cannot offer and he lets the student decide. And when a person chooses to join him in the training studio to begin to learn the martial arts, the good teacher does not simply show the student what he knows. He shares the knowledge with him and, in turn, learns from the student.

Do not be impressed by the instructor who wants to dazzle you with demonstrations of board- and brick-breaking, and give a wide berth to the instructor who hints that he has a special telephone line to the supernatural. The martial arts are natural, not supernatural. If the teacher is trying to impress you, he probably doesn't have much self-confidence.

I advise you to find a school that has attracted a variety of people. Go where you find men, women, and children with varying degrees of interest in the martial arts. Avoid schools where all the students sit around talking about the best way to bash heads. But also avoid those schools where the students spend most of their time exchanging lentil recipes and contemplating cosmic forces. A good *dojo*, like a good martial artist, has balance. It serves as a place to learn to defend yourself and to gain inner peace; it provides a program that is aimed at the body, the mind, and the spirit.

If you have any trouble finding a good school, check with one of the martial-arts magazines. Often, the editor will know of a good *dojo* in your area.

WHAT TO WEAR

Some say that when you spar in bare feet it is easier to learn good balance since more of your foot surface is in contact with the floor. I don't agree with this method. When you put shoes on the average martial artist who has never used them in training, his balance changes. Therefore, he loses his ability to kick the way he did in the training studio.

Bare feet is not real life. In ancient China, shoes were a luxury, so people went about barefooted and trained barefooted. If you're in combat in some jungle in Central America and a guy comes at you, you are not going to be able to take off your shoes so that you can kick him in the groin. You're going to be wearing heavy brogans and you'd better know how to use a technique under those real-life conditions.

A lot of guys in the martial arts do all their sparring in bare feet. If you put them into a pair of shoes, they'd have to start looking around for a tire iron or something, because their skills would be cut by 70 percent. Remember this: A martial-arts technique is no good if it works only when *you* decide where to fight, when to fight, and what to wear. Real life isn't like that. In real life, the mugger chooses the time and the place, and he's not inclined to wait while you slip into something comfortable. So you'd better be ready to fight on his terms, not your own. At my schools, we do most of our sparring with sneakers on. We figure that the only time in real life when a guy's going to be fighting in bare feet is when he's at the beach fighting to get the volleyball.

The martial-arts uniform, which is called a *gi*, is made of lightweight fabric, usually cotton. It's loose, it's comfortable, and it's what you should wear for most of your workouts. It is ideally suited to the martial arts. But the fact that it's ideal is exactly why you shouldn't wear it all the time.

If you often wear tight designer jeans outside the *dojo*, then work out in them once in a while. You should work out often in the clothes you normally wear, or else you're going to be in for a dreadful surprise some night when you learn on a dark and dangerous street that your lightning-fast punch doesn't travel quite as fast or quite as far when you are wearing a snug sports jacket, a tight collar, and a necktie. If you often wear boots, work out in them. In your martial-arts training, you must always take real life into consideration, and that includes the clothes you wear.

KATA

Kata is a Japanese word for formalized exercises. They are set routines of movement, offensive and defensive, against imaginary bad guys. The *kata* are an extremely valuable learning tool.

Like a lot of other things in the martial arts, the *kata* seem to be a dividing line between two groups of people who are wrong. On one side are the teachers who tend to treat traditional martial arts as some sort of religion instead of the practical self-defense weapon that they are. They say that *kata* are the key to the whole thing, that you cannot have martial arts without *kata*. Far on the other side there's a group of equally dogmatic individuals who say that *kata* are absolutely worthless because they don't reflect real fighting situations.

In real life, *kata* are extremely useful because they can be made to reflect authentic contemporary fighting situations, but by themselves they are not enough to create an effective fighter. *Kata* can be used to develop speed, coordination, balance, power, and precision. They can also improve technique, build endurance, and occupy the center of the mind during an active state of meditation. Unfortunately, many teachers lead students to believe that if they develop good *kata* they will be good fighters. This is not true. *Kata* is only part of your training. It must be combined with sparring and other exercises. If you just do *kata*, it is no more than a dance, and I don't have to tell you how many thieves and rapists will be scared off by a dance.

There are thousands of variations on *kata*. The combinations are infinite. Their application to a real fight is not direct, obviously, since in a real fight you do not have complete control over where the opponent stands, how he holds his weapon, or how big he is. But the *kata* you practice become a kind of vocabulary of movement. Just as you don't know the answer to a question before I ask it, you don't know what karate technique is applicable until the situation exists. But practicing *kata* is a form of studying. It helps you to come up with the right answer quickly when you need it.

Incidentally, if you'd like to play music while you go through your *kata*, that's fine. But play music that gives you the rhythm you need in fighting. Do not play hard, pulsating, disturbing rock music, or distracting vocals.

DEVELOPING STRENGTH AND POWER

Strength is not the most important asset of the martial artist, but neither is it something you can neglect. You can practice techniques for a lifetime, but if you do not build strength, your techniques might amount to nothing.

Yes, it is true that the 90-pound girl who has a black belt could quickly defeat the 210-pound stevedore who knows no technique. But if the stevedore is also a black belt, the girl had better start looking for an exit. When martial artists of equal skill and knowledge meet, strength becomes the determining factor. (The exception to this generalization would be when two superior martial artists or grand masters face each other. Then the weaker one won't necessarily lose. The one who makes the first mistake will lose.)

So in your martial arts training, work diligently on building your strength. This does not mean that you have to pump iron daily and develop huge knots of muscle up and down your arms. To develop inner strength and outer strength, do breathing exercises, isometrics, and isotonics. Isometric exercises are those that contract the muscles through resistance without moving, such as pushing against a wall or any other immovable object. Isotonics are exercises against an object where there is some resistance but there is movement, such as lifting weights.

While developing your strength in general, you will also work on strengthening specific parts of your body. For example, in order to use effectively the iron palm and iron fist techniques, which we'll discuss later, you must work hard on increasing the strength in your fingers, palms, wrists, and forearms. Also, there are specific exercises and stances for strengthening the legs.

To develop strong hands and powerful punches, stand in a horse stance (legs apart as if you are straddling a horse) and punch out your right fist in front of you. *Kiai* as you punch out. Repeat this with the left fist, several times (after you have warmed up). Imagine that you have the most devastating and powerful punch in the universe. Use your mind to direct your internal energy to flow into the tip of your fist. Do this punching exercise until you are tired. After a few months you will notice a distinct increase in your strength and you will acquire an extremely powerful punch.

You can also punch and hit heavy bags, light bags, and speed bags without wearing gloves. This will help toughen hands. Another great exercise for developing a powerful punch is to hold a small dumbbell in each hand and punch.

To develop strength and power in the fingers and hands, do poking, clawing, and thrusting strikes with the fingers and palms into a bucket of sand. After you have been training for a couple of weeks, gradually mix the sand with small stones and repeat the procedure. Also do push-ups and pull-ups using just the fingers. This will strengthen them. Squeeze a small ball in the palm of your hand for ten seconds at a time. Breathe in as you squeeze, exhale as you release. This builds power in the hand and arm.

REFLEX TRAINING

The typical martial-arts training program includes short, quick combinations of moves known as reflex training. A combination is usually two or more moves, with speed as the critical factor. If a *kata* is a story, then a combination is a sentence.

Reflex training is used to develop quick responses to situations, particularly situations that come up suddenly, such as the arrival of an attacker's knife in your line of vision. A good teacher will make you practice many moves. In real life, the first move is the most important. If you don't get to use it, there's not going to be a second move, and there might not even be a tomorrow. Speed is the most important element of the first move. Here are some exercises you can do at home to get an idea of what reflex training is all about.

Hold a sheet of paper straight out in front of you with one hand, or have a friend hold it. Now bring your other hand from fully relaxed to explosive and try to poke your fingers through the paper. You probably won't be able to at first. You'll just knock the paper out of the way. But when you've developed enough speed and that immediate explosive power that comes when you blank out your mind, your fingers will bore holes through the paper.

Here's another reflex drill. Be careful with this one. Light a tall candle and place it on a table. Now try to punch out the flame without touching the candle. The trick is to stop just short

106

of the flame while the vacuum created by your fist pulling back puts out the flame.

Here's another exercise. Blow up a balloon and toss it in the air. When it's just a foot or two from the floor, kick it up again. Try to keep it airborne with your kicks. This is a little harder than it sounds because the balloon floats away from you. You'll develop speed in getting to the balloon before it touches the floor. As you loosen you'll see that your foot is going higher and higher to meet the balloon, and if you count the number of kicks each time, you'll see that number rising steadily over the months of your training.

PUNCH FROM THE HEEL

In the martial arts there is a useful concept known as the *ki*. The *ki* is supposed to be the invisible energy that flows through your body from all points in the universe. You can tap into this energy to increase speed, power, and overall effectiveness. Typically, the martial artist will use visualization techniques, such as the ones we talked about earlier, to utilize the *ki*.

Most karate instructors tell their students that the center for the *ki* is an imaginary point just below the navel. That is approximately the center of gravity for the human body, so they recommend striking from that point. They reason that if the *ki* is in the center of the body, then it is in the center of the universe. But in real life, if we assume an infinite universe, then all points are the center. Perhaps we should take our eyes off the universe for a second and take another look at the human body.

I believe in using every part of the body when I strike. I don't punch from the shoulder or the waist. I punch from the heel. If I bring all my power up through my legs and torso and channel it into my hand, I am hitting with my whole body. The source of maximum power is not in the navel; it's in the heel. To get the most power, weight distribution, and transfer, the blow should come from the heel. You can perhaps get the feel of this through some visualization. Imagine that your heel is a volcano. When you are ready to strike, let the volcano erupt and spew its power up through your body.

BREAKING BRICKS AND BOARDS

One of the most commonly seen images of the martial arts is the breaking of bricks or boards with a sudden explosive chop. The practice is flashy and leaves an imprint on the public mind, but it's hardly what you would call essential to the martial artist. And if it's taken too seriously, it can be extremely harmful.

This vandalism against inanimate objects is usually done in demonstrations to show the power of karate. If it helps to draw people into the martial arts, that's fine. I'm for it. However, it is also used by teachers to impress potential students, and that, it seems to me, is a bit dishonest.

In the first place, to tell you the truth, breaking bricks and boards isn't one of the harder things you'll have to do in the martial arts. The guys who give these demonstrations are usually pretty good chefs. If they're going to break a few boards, they cook them up in the oven ahead of time. This baking draws the excess moisture out of the wood, and that, combined with the fact that our mighty man smashes the wood in the direction of the grain, makes board-breaking relatively easy. If our hero is going to show us how severely he can punish a couple of bricks, you can be certain that he's gotten hold of bricks with the highest possible sand content. The more sand a brick contains, the easier it is to break.

These demonstrations by themselves don't hurt anybody, and they make for good showmanship. But they can put an inappropriate emphasis on the breaking of bricks and boards in martial-arts training. Martial-arts books and instructors often advise board- and brick-breaking as a way to toughen up the hands for chops. This is ridiculous, unnecessary, and dangerous. The human body is one of the softest things you are ever going to strike, and to do it effectively you don't have to have a pair of hands that look like catcher's mitts.

The fact is that a lot of brick- and board-breaking will take away more than it gives. Toughened, callused hands tend to rob the all-important fingers of mobility, and they often become arthritic. My advice? After you've been training for a while and you understand the principles of concentration, no-mind, and punching for a thousand miles, break a few boards to prove you can do it. Get it out of your system, and then forget about it.

One last word of caution: Don't ever try to break bricks and boards with your head. That's not going to prove anything. You can end up with serious, even fatal, head injuries.

A GOOD WORKOUT

At the risk of sounding like a missionary for the martial arts, I'm going to say it:

A MARTIAL ARTS PROGRAM IS THE BEST EXERCISE PROGRAM IN THE WORLD!

A martial-arts program incorporates the stretching, the constant level of resistance, and the attention to the whole body, which are the hallmarks of a practical and healthful exercise program. And the emphasis on the alert mind and the calm body adds immeasurably to all-around good health.

I'm going to offer you my recommendation for a good workout. But first, there are two things you should keep in mind. Number one: Do not overexercise. Take it easy at first. Your endurance will grow naturally; you don't have to force it. Whatever you can do today you will be able to do more of next week. Don't push yourself to prove a point. Exercise should leave you invigorated, not exhausted. And point number two: Before you start any new physical-fitness program you should visit a doctor. Get a physical exam, find out what kind of shape you are in. Chances are it's not so bad.

I work out four hours every day seven days a week. That's not so hard for me to schedule; it's part of my workday. It's like a welder welding four hours a day. But few people can put in four hours every day. So I'll just divide my plan into four periods and you can prorate it over your exercise time, which should be at least an hour. Incidentally, you do have an hour a day you can spare for exercise, even if you think you don't. Get up an hour earlier if you have to. An hour in the morning is worth three in the afternoon. If you exercise first thing in the morning, you will get more done in the next seven hours than you would ordinarily accomplish in ten. You'll feel great all day.

So get up early. Don't eat before you exercise. Walk around, loosen up, stretch. Now you're ready. For the first period begin with stretching exercises, then move on to calisthenics and strength-building exercises such as weightlifting; also do some isometrics.

During the second period practice kicks from different stances. Don't try to be competitive and beat yesterday's performance. Just do your best. Improvement will come.

During the third period work on *katas*. This is extremely relaxing. Use it as meditative time and you will feel peaceful and in control throughout the day.

During the fourth period practice sparring and sparring techniques.

Do a four-part workout like this every day. It is better to substitute sections than to try to cover everything in one session. For example, eliminate the *kata* one day and work on knife techniques, or take out the kicking section and replace it with a period of punching.

When I talk about sparring techniques, I'm also talking about bag work and punching and kicking into the air. You kick or punch into the air to develop speed. However, and this is very important, do not make any movements into the air at full power. When you have resistance, such as a punching bag, then full power is fine. The resistance creates balance. But this business of flailing away at the air full power for training is foolish, and it hurts your body.

Some martial-arts instructors have people whacking away at nothing at full power and not thinking about the future at all. Three years later, those people are like little old men. They've got weak elbows, weak knees, and weak backs because when you are using full power and not hitting anything, the pressure goes back to the joints and weakens the body. That's real life.

The whole point of exercise is to enjoy the physical and mental benefits of it, not to ruin your body. You have to pace yourself in exercise, just as you have to pace yourself in life. So when you punch or kick into the air, use 50 percent power. Balance! And when you want to punch full power, use a bag. And when you want to kick full power, *use* a dummy, don't *be* a dummy.

BASIC STRETCHES

Tiger Reaches for the Sky Front Stretch

1. Start with your left leg in front of you and your right leg as far back as possible.
2. Bend your front leg, keeping your rear leg as straight as possible with your weight on the ball of your rear foot.
3. Keep the knee of your back leg off the ground.
4. Raise your hands over your head, palms extended and fingers clenched.
5. Arch your back and look toward the sky.
6. Slowly, raise and lower your body by bending your front leg.
7. Alternate to stretch both legs.

This exercise is used to stretch the upper thigh of the rear leg and the upper muscles of the front leg. It is also good for developing balance.

111

Dragon Stretches Its Tail

1. Start with your feet wide apart.
2. Bend your right knee, keeping your left leg straight.
3. Slowly, go as low as possible while keeping your left foot flat on the floor.
4. Alternate from side to side, approximately thirty times.

NOTE: The amount of times that you alternate will depend on your physical capabilities.

This exercise is used for the inner groin muscles, the inner thigh, and, partially, for the hip area.

Leopard Loosens Its Joints

1. Have a seat on the floor.
2. Put your right leg forward and your left leg back.
3. Keep your right leg straight and bend your left leg at the knee.
4. Slide your left leg as far back as possible.
5. Bend forward and try to touch your chin to your right knee.
6. Alternate.

This exercise stretches the back of the forward leg and, partially, the inner groin muscles.

Advanced Leopard Loosens Its Joints Stretch

1. Squat down so that you are sitting on the heel of your left leg.
2. Extend your right leg straight out.
3. Bend foward.
4. Touch your chin to your extended leg or to the floor in front of you.
5. Alternate.

Crane Stretches for Water

1. Start in a standing position with feet about one and a half shoulders' width apart.
2. Cross your arms in front of your chest.
3. Slowly, bend forward at the waist toward the floor.
4. Let your arms and head hang down.
5. If your elbows can touch the floor, bring your feet closer together.

This exercise stretches the hamstrings (backs of the legs) and the lower back.

Cat Stretch

1. Start with your hands and feet on the floor, heels as close to the ground as possible.
2. Tuck your head in toward your knees without moving your hands.
3. Bend your arms, straighten your back, and keep your nose close to the floor.
4. Push forward. Then raise your head up. Straighten your arms, arch your back, and look upward.
5. To begin again, drop your head and chest. Bend your arms. Nose close to the floor, push back and up to position 1. Breathe in on the way up, breathe out on the way down.

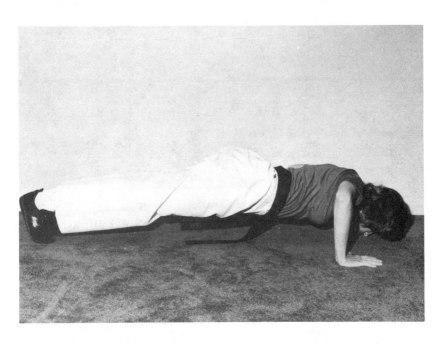

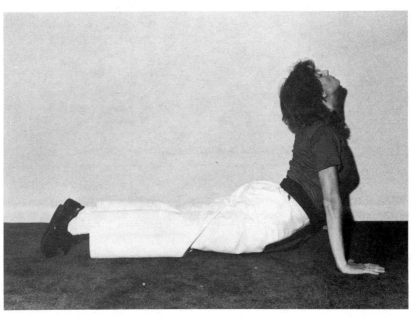

117

An Isometric Exercise

Using the wall for resistance, push against it in various positions. By changing positions you will strengthen different muscle groups. Hold each position for ten seconds. Then release. Repeat each five times.

Wall Stretches

In order to do these stretches, place your leg upon an object, such as a chair or a desk, and for the advanced version, high on a wall.

This stretch is done from both a forward stance and a side stance. Done from a forward stance, this exercise will stretch the back of your leg. From a side stance, you will stretch the inner thigh area.

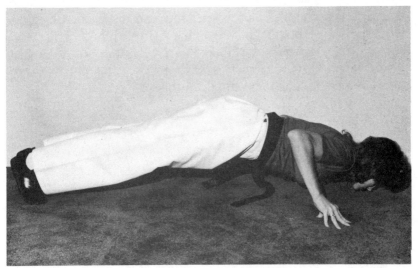

Finger Tip Push-ups

These exercises are used to develop strength in fingers, hands, and forearms. They are used to add strength to the Poison Hand and to various clawing and raking techniques.

119

STRIKES AND KICKS

For the following pages I have selected a few strikes and kicks and demonstrated ways in which they can be delivered. They are fairly simple and you can practice them at home as part of your training, though you won't truly master them until you have worked on them in a *dojo* with a trained instructor to help you.

Though we generally think of striking with the hands and kicking with the feet in straight lines, keep in mind that the trained martial artist can attack with almost any part of the body. There are as many ways to strike as your body has ways to move, bend, twist, turn, and thrust.

The strikes and kicks you will use will depend on your size, the size of your opponent, the distance between you and your opponent, and on which strikes and kicks you feel you have developed proficiency. At a distance you might use, for example, the Poison Hand strike of the snake. In close you might go to the powerful elbow and knee strikes of the crane.

In a real fight, strikes and kicks must be delivered with speed and power. However, as you begin to practice the strikes and kicks in this section, do not worry about speed. Speed will come. Concentrate on being able to deliver these blows while still maintaining your balance. That is far more important. A fast and powerful blow that costs you your balance is not worth it. Your balance is your most important asset.

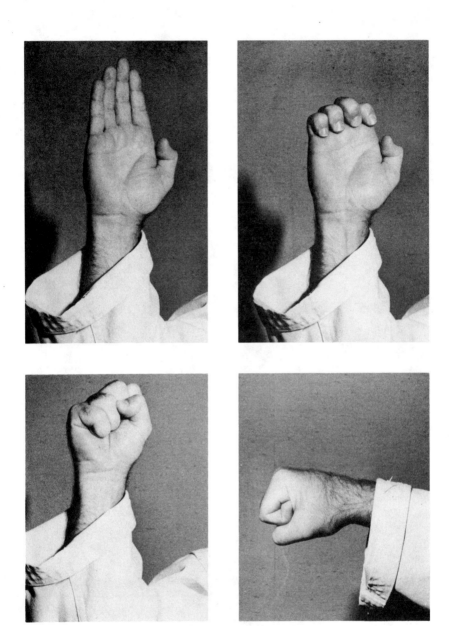

How to Make a Proper Fist

1. Start with your palm open.
2. Bend all fingers at the second joint.
3. Bend all fingers at the third joint.
4. Place your thumb over the first two fingers and clench.

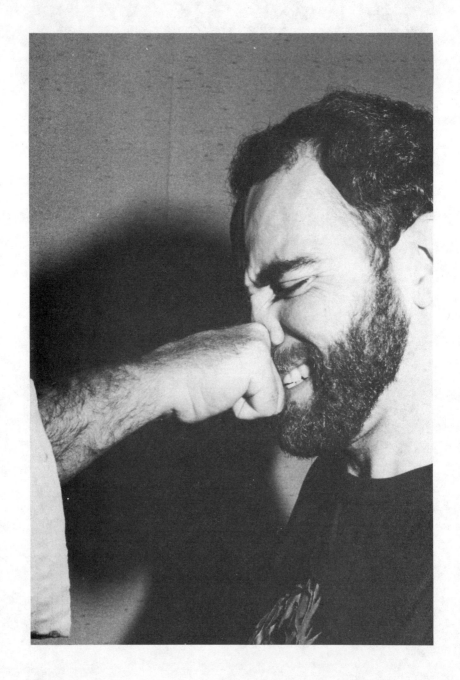

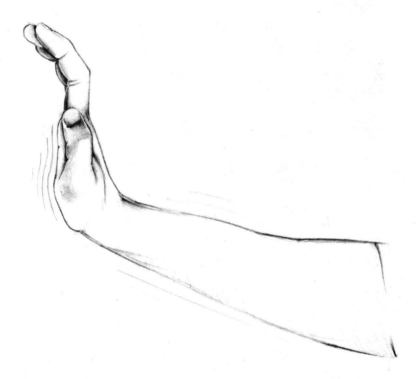

The Palm Heel

To Form a Palm Heel:

1. Open your palm wide.
2. Tuck your thumb in.
3. Keep your fingers close together and slightly bent.
4. Bend your wrist back so that your fingers are pointing upward and the heel of your hand is extended.

This strike is used to areas such as the ribs, cheekbone, chin, nose, back, head, and heart.

Here is a Thrusting Palm Heel delivered to the heart of an attacker.

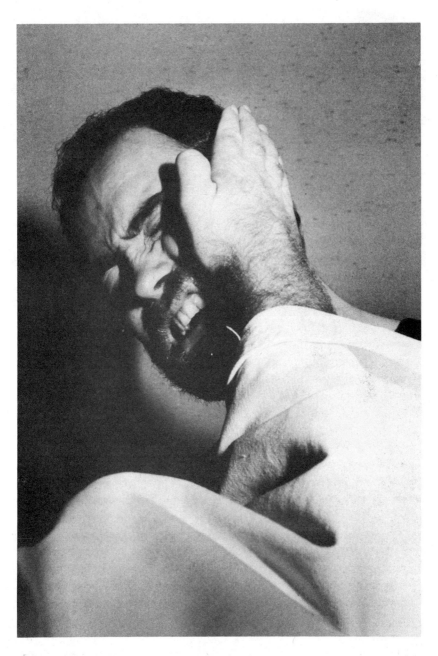

The Willow Palm is delivered in a circular motion. It is often used to the cheekbone, the temple, and the ear.

Crescent Kick—Reverse Crescent

This is a circular, straight-legged kick delivered in front of your body. The striking surface can be either the inside or outside of your foot. It is often used to kick weapons out of an opponent's hand or away from the line of your body, allowing you time for a follow-up technique.

The crescent is very useful for kicking at close range.

Target areas are the head, groin, hands, and arms.

Bow Kick

The Bow Kick is a devastating kick that can be delivered at close range.

It is a short, circular kick using the middle portion of the leg, between the knee and foot, to strike with.

Excellent target areas for this kick are the rib cage, kidneys, and thighs.

Front Heel Kick

Excellent for kicking in close range, this kick is used for the groin and the midsection. It can also be used for the head.

NOTE: Although kicking high is good to do, it is more important to maintain balance throughout your kick.

1. To start, stand in a horse stance for practice. This gives you the ability to practice with both left and right feet.

2. Flamingo. Bring kicking foot to opposite knee, forming position of foot in this step. Keep the leg you are standing on bent for stability.

3. Extension. Thrust leg, exploding upward and outward toward
a chosen target; keep heel extended throughout kick.

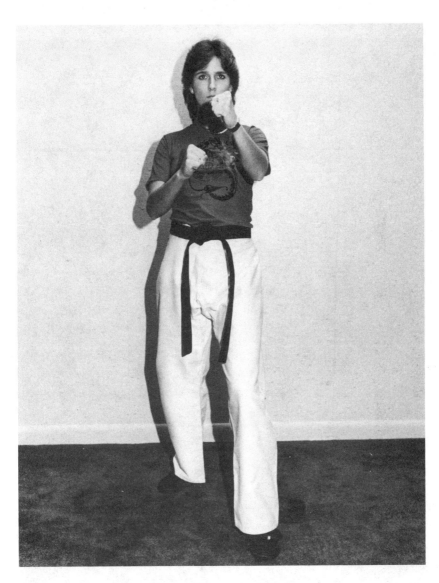

Roundhouse Kick

This kick could be used as a defense to an aggressive attacker by stepping to the side and delivering toward the midsection, using the instep or the ball of the foot as your striking surface.

Used offensively, this kick is directed to the side of the knee, rib cage, heart, or temple.

1. Begin in a normal fighting stance.

2. Bring knee high, pivoting the foot you are standing on approximately ninety degrees.

134

3. Extend the lower part of your leg, striking with either the instep or the ball of your foot.

Side Snap Kick

This kick can be delivered with a quick "snap" motion using the blade edge of the foot, or a more powerful thrusting motion by using the bottom of the foot—the Side Thrust Kick. This means the kick could "cut" a joint, quickly "slap" a vulnerable area, or act as a battering ram, devastating and disguised.

Some of the various striking areas are the knee, groin, rib cage, solar plexus, and throat.

1. Start in a side horse stance for practice, with the hands directed to the side for stability and guard.

   NOTE: The Side Kick can also be delivered from a forward stance.

136

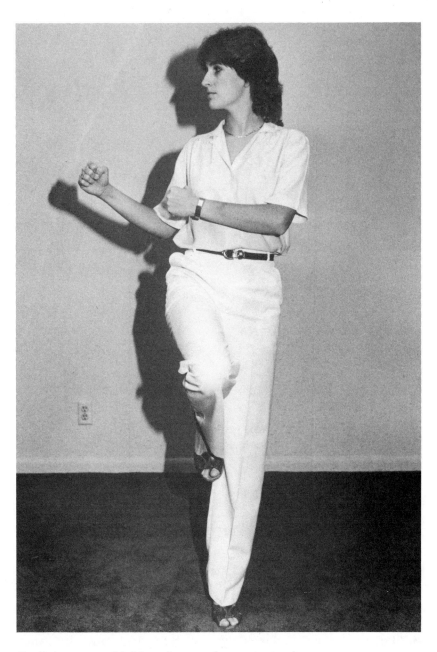

2. Bring your kicking foot to the opposite knee.

3. Raise the knee high with your kicking foot moving toward your opponent and your base foot pivoting slightly.

4. Extend the leg with the heel higher than the toes, forming a blade with the foot.

Dragon Tail Kick "Wheel Kick"

This kick is a spinning, circular one that utilizes the weight of the entire body. The leg as well as the foot is used as the striking surface.

The object of this kick is to hit and move circularly through your opponent, thus causing him to lose his balance.

The Dragon Tail Kick is excellent for use to the midsection, back, sides, and head. It is also excellent for a rushing attacker.

1. Begin from a normal fighting stance.

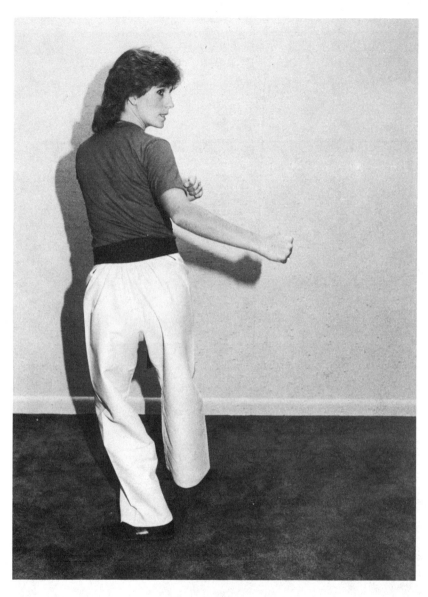

Begin Spin

2. Shift weight to lead leg and begin rotation with upper body.
Lift kicking leg straight toward side of opponent. (From what
your opponent believes is a position of weakness, you grasp
victory in an instant.)

Just Before Impact

3. Maintain circular motion with the entire body allowing leg to follow through opponent.

Impact and Follow-through

4. Pivot the foot you are standing on a complete 360 degrees, returning kicking leg to the original starting position.

Follow-through

5. The following move to this kick is often a spinning-hand
   technique using the flowing movements of the dragon to
   submission.

Back Kick

This kick may be delivered either at close range or at more of a distance. It is the most powerful kick delivered from a standing position and may be used successfully to the groin, midsection, or head.

1. Begin in a horse stance for practice. It may also be delivered from a normal fighting stance in defense situations.

2. Bring foot up to knee with most of the foot behind the knee.
   Pull toes back and extend heel. Hit your target with the heel,
   not the bottom of your foot.

3. Move upper body forward slightly while thrusting heel backward.

NOTE: The secret of the follow-up of all kicking technique is balance.

DIET

I am very proud and happy to take this opportunity to announce to the world the fabulous new Fred Villari Diet. It's a guaranteed weight-loss diet with no adverse side effects, no expensive supplements, no special equipment, and no complicated schedules. It goes like this:

To lose weight eat less food and get more exercise.

Not very radical, is it? That's the point. Let's face it, unless you've been living in a cave for the past twenty years, you already know how to lose weight. Everybody knows how to lose weight. There have been thousands of books published, and millions of articles, TV shows, and pamphlets. We're all grown-ups here, so let's not pretend that there is some great secret to the whole thing. There is practically no adult in this country who doesn't know that exercise will burn up calories and that overeating causes excessive weight gain, that fruits and vegetables are good for you and that sugar, pastry, cokes, and coffee are not so good. It's not complicated, and it's not magical or secret. Everybody knows most of the facts, and anybody who is overweight and does not drop some of those pounds, quite simply, is not making an honest effort.

Certainly you can lose weight by limiting yourself to sprout soup, celery sticks, and an occasional grape. But why go on living under those conditions? As far as I'm concerned, your diet should consist of balanced proportions, and the simplest way to lose weight is to take what you normally eat and cut it in half. Eat what you want: ice cream, whatever, but cut it in half. I like to keep it simple.

The martial arts are a highly effective vehicle for weight loss. I'd say 10 percent of the people who come to my studios are trying to lose weight. Obviously the program burns calories, but I don't think that's the main reason for its effectiveness in reducing weight and eliminating fat. The mental and spiritual aspects of the martial arts are the real keys. You learn discipline, which you can then apply to your eating habits. You improve your appearance, and you want to improve it even more by getting rid of fat. And most of all, you begin to feel good—very good—about yourself, and you no longer want to treat your body poorly with a lot of unhealthful food.

As for drugs and smoking, it's the same story. Don't kid yourself. I know that drugs and smoking are bad for your health, and you know they are bad for your health. The whole world knows they are bad for your health. It's no secret. I do not smoke or use street drugs of any kind, and if you are serious about the martial arts, you won't either.

SPARRING

When we talk about sparring, most people think of boxing. In fact, the term *sparring* is even more appropriate for the martial arts because it comes from the Italian word *sparare,* which means, among other things, to kick. In martial-arts sparring you kick, punch, block, trap, hold, and do everything else you would do in a real fight, except you do it without trying to inflict serious harm.

To see the wisdom of using sparring in training we need look no further than the animals. Baby bears, baby lions, and other baby animals learn to hunt and do battle through relatively harmless play. The animal kingdom is full of mock fights that prepare the animal for real-life battles.

There are three types of sparring: noncontact, light contact, and full contact. In noncontact sparring you don't touch your opponent. You stop short of your target. If you are sparring for points, you score according to what you could have done.

After you have reached the rank of black belt, you progress to controlled-contact (light-contact) sparring, hitting your man without excessive contact. For example, you land a good knife hand to the ribs, but stop short just as you land the blow. All you need is the feeling of contact to learn gauging. I train my black belts to make a certain amount of contact as they go up the black-belt ranks.

Sparring is an adventure. Some people are more adventurous than others. There is no need to begin sparring before the rank of purple, blue, or even green belt. However, in my schools we teach sparring *exercises* from ten feet away after the second week of training, and then we bring the student closer as he progresses.

Sparring is your first major step in eliminating fear and ego.

You become familiar with fear-inspiring situations, such as kicks and punches whizzing past your head. You learn that being afraid does you no good. You discard the fear. Sparring is an indispensable part of your training. It develops fighting skills and helps you to erase the flaws in your technique. Also, you learn a good deal from your sparring partners.

But keep a couple of things in mind. One, sparring is an attempt to bring you and your martial-arts skills closer to real-life situations. But it is not a perfect reflection of real life. For example, in point sparring you could throw a kick and score a point even though you fell down afterward. In real life if you throw a kick and fall down, you don't score a point, you get stomped on. In the training studio your opponent does not intend to rob, rape, or kill you. In real life he might.

Also, in real life you would aim for vital points. Do not aim for vital points in sparring. It's true that the advanced martial artist can release a powerful blow and stop just short of a guy's vital point, leaving a space no thicker than a maple leaf. But this is no game of chicken, and there's no point in endangering a fellow martial artist's health just to see if you could have poked his eyes out. I believe in training only black belts and above in making substantial contact. It makes the situation more realistic.

Full-contact karate is more of a controlled situation than free sparring because you can only use certain techniques. In full-contact karate the fighters load themselves up with enough padding to insulate a small house, and they go at it.

Of course, if they made the pads thinner, you'd see a lot of interesting fighting. The only problem is that a lot of people would get killed.

LEARNING

The role of the teacher in the martial arts cannot be overrated. A good martial-arts instructor can save you years of poor training habits. He can help you to find your strengths and neutralize your weaknesses. He can help you to continually widen your repertoire of technique. He can provide you with encouragement and wisdom.

But that is not enough. If you only know what you learn from your teacher, you will be limited by his knowledge. In real life you must also be a self-teacher. You must learn from you.

Overall, the martial-arts instructor has a pretty decent public image, and I think it's well deserved. He's healthy, wise, peaceful; a guy who doesn't go looking for trouble, but knows what to do if trouble shows up. That's fair. Most martial-arts instructors are creative, forward-looking people with a zest for life and a sincere love of the martial arts. This translates into enthusiasm for their work and their students. But let's face it, in real life there are stiffs in every profession, and it would be dishonest of me to pretend that the martial-arts world doesn't have its share.

One character that you find in the martial arts is the guy who leaped into the arts with both feet years ago. He was enthusiastic, energetic, and hardworking. He sucked up whatever information was available, acquired a black belt, and moved up a few degrees. But, like his counterparts in any field you can name, he got tired, lazy, complacent, too easily satisfied. He stopped growing. So he got himself hooked up with some karate federation. He joined so that he and the other guys there could swap diplomas and certify each other's skills. This guy hasn't learned anything new in thirty years. His mind has calcified. And when the student comes to him with a new idea, he says, "It can't be done," like the burned-out doctor who says, "There's no cure for that."

Well, a guy like this can teach you a lot if you're just starting out. But don't get stuck where he is. Don't be the kind of student who can't learn anything unless his teacher gives it to him. You must develop the mind of a master on your own. The master sees through things; he can stare straight through a technique and see the better way. If you develop the outlook, the attitude of a master, you will find in your own mind a vast array of techniques. Deep within your own mind and soul lie the answers to many questions not yet asked.

Do not try to be just as good as your teacher. Try to be better. If students do not surpass their teachers, the martial arts as a whole will not grow.

VII

FIGHTING STRATEGY

Outlined in this section are the various steps in fighting strategy: I take you in sequence from the beginning to the end of the fight.

EVALUATING YOUR OPPONENT

While you are gauging—setting your distance—evaluate your opponent carefully. Look for his strengths and weaknesses. It is more important to be able to determine and see clearly his strengths than his weaknesses. If you are wrong in judging your opponent's strengths, you may lose the battle. If you are wrong in judging his weaknesses, you should not get into too much trouble.

GAUGING

Often, people estimate badly the distance between themselves and their opponent, so most people fight at a distance that is too far to be effective. They assume it is safer. The problem with fighting at too great a distance is that you can telegraph your movements from an attacking or defending position, allowing your opponent to see your movements too easily.

For the trained fighter, gauging properly is maneuvering at a distance great enough so that your opponent cannot reach the main part of your body with a punch or kick. The main portion, or middle section, of your body is harder to move out of the way of a punch or kick. You can bring your head back six to nine inches, you can slide your legs to the side, but the middle portion stays.

STANCES AND FIGHTING

In your martial-arts training you'll be shown a lot of classic stances. The horse stance, for example, is one in which the fighter stands with his legs spread apart and his knees bent as if he is straddling a horse. This stance is excellent for developing balance. It also builds body strength, particularly in the legs. But it's for training, not for fighting.

If you wanted to be the aggressor and you began in a horse stance, you would put yourself at a great disadvantage because you'd have to bring your body and weight around before you could attack an opponent the way you should. Or you could attack with just one side of your body, which would cause your attack to be very weak. You would not be able to put all of your weight into your strike, bury the punch, or seal the kick.

Another stance, the traditional wide fighting stance, can get you into even more difficulty. In real life if you come up against a vicious street fighter and you get down into a low wide stance, you'd better hope he didn't bring a baseball bat along for the festivities, because whacking your knee with the bat will be as easy as swiping a fly off the kitchen table.

If your feet are spread too far apart, it will be very hard to adjust and move quickly. Also, a stance that is too wide exposes your feet and legs to your opponent for takedown, felling techniques, and scoops.

The ideal fighting stance would be to have the heels of your feet directly under your shoulders. This stance gives you greater maneuverability and mobility. It allows you to shift your weight more quickly, thus making it easier to shuffle or slide, to move laterally, or to use circular techniques. Also, because your feet are already under you and your weight is more centered, you don't have to bring your feet in to move. Once your feet have been positioned at the correct distance apart, you should place the weak side of your body closest to your opponent. This means that if you are a right-handed puncher or kicker, your weaker left side should be closest to your opponent and your right side farthest away. Having the right side back would enable you to put all of your weight and power into the technique. You should of course work toward not having a weak side. If you can keep switching, you can confuse your opponent even more.

Forward Leaning Stance

Weight distribution:
60% rear foot
40% front foot

Cat Stance

Weight distribution:
90% rear foot
10% front foot

Back Leaning Stance
Weight distribution:
80% rear foot
20% front foot

159

Normal Fighting Stance

Weight distribution:
50% rear foot
50% front foot

The position of your hands should be as follows: Your lead hand should be farthest from your body, and below your eyes so it won't block your vision. Your rear hand should be positioned closer to the body. The elbow of the rear hand should be no more than four inches from the body. Your rear hand should also be six inches lower than your lead hand. This makes the body a much harder target to hit. Also, this fighting position allows you to use all parts of your body to block, both feet to kick, and both hands to punch. This stance is superior to other stances when used against blocking, punching, or kicking because it utilizes the entire body. It is much easier to trap, deflect, or lock the opponent's hands or feet from this position.

THE STARE

Your eyes must always look through your opponent's, not into them. Your eyes should never wander. They should be slightly narrowed.

HEAD POSITION

Your head should be held erect and should be clear of confusing thoughts. If you have too many thoughts, you can lose the fight. Let your head be clear so that you will remember and use all your fighting knowledge. When your mind is clear you can easily adapt to the situation and change to the technique that will defeat the enemy. Don't move, bob, or weave the head when facing the opponent. When your opponent attacks, you can move your head in any direction, or bob and weave.

POSTURE

Your posture in fighting will vary depending on your size and shape. You should try to keep your spine as straight as possible because you can deliver foot and hand combinations more quickly from that position than from a crouching or leaning position. Because your body is already straight and free, you don't go through the wasted motion of having to untangle and un-knot your extremities. It is much harder for your opponent to try to figure what you are going to do next from this posture. Your body will not give you away when you attack.

FIGHTING ATTITUDE

A good fighting attitude is essential. It will greatly influence the outcome of the fight. And if your opponent has equal skills, knowledge, and strength, attitude will probably be the deciding factor. Your attitude should be that you love to fight, you fight to win, and you would die before you would quit.

STARTING THE ATTACK

Whether you start the attack or your opponent starts the attack, it doesn't matter. Most of the time it will depend on what type of fighter you are: aggressive, defensive, or offensive. It will be easier to defeat your opponent once he has started the attack. You can easily see his weaknesses because he's in motion and, most of the time, off-balance.

Not that it is wrong for you to be the aggressor. Sometimes it is better to be the aggressor. If you have quick reflexes and excellent footwork, you can be the aggressor and it will work to your advantage.

Whether you should be aggressive or defensive will depend on your situation. Knowing which way is correct each time is something to study and think about.

MOVEMENT AND FIGHTING

When you fight correctly, you don't jerk your arms and legs around like a robot. You move as naturally as you move when taking an afternoon stroll. The best movements are the natural movements. Lions and tigers don't change the flow of their motion when trouble comes along, so why should you? You've spent your life learning movements that are natural and efficient, so don't abandon them when you see two weirdos skulk-ing down the alley at you. That's when you most need natural movement. Your head should move like a monkey, your body should float like a dragon, and when you strike you should be as deeply rooted as the tallest tree.

FOOTWORK

Once you have learned to bob, weave, shuffle, slip, dodge, and slide, it will be almost impossible for your opponent to lay a hand on you. And when you have confidence in your footwork, you will be relaxed and secure about using any technique you want.

In your training you will learn that small steps and shuffles, forward, backward, and lateral, are essential in fighting. When your opponent comes in to deliver a kick or a punch, shuffle back six inches so that you are out of the way until you are able to counter. But remember, the farther you run from your opponent, the harder it is for you to execute that counter move. And the farther you dodge to the side, the more vulnerable you are to be opened up for a kicking technique. So get out of the way, but not by more than you have to.

In fighting, footwork is more important than kicking and punching. If you are fast on your feet, you can always get away. Even if you are a slow puncher but fast-footed, you can move in to your opponent's body without getting hit, deliver your slow punch, and get out of the way without getting damaged. The ultimate goal, of course, is to have fast and agile leg move-ments, a quick punch, and a kick that makes lightning look slow. By switching back and forth from fighting flat-footed to stand-ing on the balls of your feet, you can shuffle, bob, duck, slide, or dip without turning or twisting your body, and without tele-graphing your moves. Remember, if your next move is predict-able, chances are it won't work because your opponent can find its weakness.

The best fighter is the one who slips his techniques through while his opponent is striking or moving. To do this he comes very close to his attacker's strikes or kicks, but remains elusive. You must strive to become the person who cannot be touched.

BREAK THE BALANCE

Every time you kick or punch, try to put your opponent off-balance before you strike, as you strike, and after you strike.

When you've hit an opponent, always try to use your feet to move your opponent's feet in order to break his balance. You can break his balance by pushing him, pulling him, trapping him or redirecting him, tripping him, shoving him, or throwing him. Take your pick.

Also, any time an opponent kicks or uses his feet, you should immediately try to break his balance. You can do this by using your hands to trap or by using your feet to change the direction of his feet.

CONFUSE THE MIND

Normally, when someone is fighting, he makes the mistake of trying to hit the same area over and over. The wise martial artist goes to where he is least expected. Never throw a punch or a kick to the same part of the body in two consecutive strikes. If your first punch goes to the head, the opponent's reflexes send out the alarm—head under attack—and his hands fly up to block his head before you get there the second time. Let his reflexes work for you. Always deliver the second blow to another part of the body. For example, if you punch to the head with the left, your right punch should go to the midsection, then follow it up with the left punch back to the head, then the right hand to another part of the body. This confuses the opponent so that his reflexes cannot take over.

This also applies to kicking. If, for example, you are kicking to the rib cage on the right side of your opponent's body, don't follow it with a punch to the rib cage. His reflexes are rushing to protect that part of the body and he's going to be fading to the opposite direction away from your punch. So your second technique should be from the other side of your body, and you can catch him off-balance. If you work different parts of your opponent's body, it will be easier for you to catch him off-balance.

So, to confuse your opponent, punch then grapple, kick then punch, circle the body, continually surprise him; never do the obvious, the expected. Never attack head on unless you are much stronger. Alternate target areas. Keep moving, striking, hitting, and shifting your weight until that moment when you know that there is one kick or punch or holding technique that will finish him off.

SPINNING TECHNIQUES

Any time you use a spinning technique, first fake to the opposite side of your opponent's body before you spin. A fake is a throw of a punch or a kick that is held back. It will trick your opponent and also get you started on your move inward. The fake will make your opponent move in the direction that you are going to spin out of. Use the spinning technique just as his body is starting to move from the fake, and you'll catch him off-balance. If, for example, you are facing your opponent with your left foot forward and you want to deliver a right-handed spinning backfist, you are going to spin clockwise. To be effective you should first throw a fake kick or punch to get his body moving counterclockwise a few inches. Remember that when your opponent starts to move, his balance is weakened. You can use spinning techniques without faking a move, but you must have quicker reflexes than the opponent you are fighting. This is because a spinning technique takes up a long moment and leaves your back exposed.

ATTACKS AND COUNTERATTACKS

The attack should be learned equally as well as the counterattack because if you are fighting more than one opponent, you are much more successful if you use both. If you are standing still and have many attacking you at once, you are left vulnerable. You become a stationary target.

However, when you attack, you become more off-balance than the person who is waiting to be attacked. When you move in to attack, you create many movements and positions that your opponent can easily counter. You expose yourself and show your move first because you are moving—hands, feet, or body—and thus creating an opening for your opponent to land a blow somewhere on your body and ultimately annihilate you.

My advice to those individuals who like to use the attack: Attack only if you feel as though your reflexes are much faster than your opponent's. If you are a slow mover, puncher, or kicker, I advise you to wait and be the counterattacker.

In counterattacking you should not move at all until the last moment. This gives you more time to think and react, thus you will not make any errors or create easy openings for the attacker.

If you are being attacked by many, use both the attack and counterattack. You must keep your movements flowing so that you are not easily pinned or trapped. If you are attacked by one opponent, you can wait until he comes to you. But whether you are the attacker or counterattacker, when you start your move or when it is your turn to move, *do not stop moving, flowing, punching, throwing, kicking, trapping, or sliding until your opponent is on the ground and subdued.*

I do not believe that after a fight begins (as in traditional systems) there should be pauses between attacks or counterattacks of flurries of kicks or punches. After you attack or counterattack, the fight should not last more than ten seconds. Accept and believe this and you will not find yourself rolling and brawling on the ground like some drunk.

FIGHTING IN CLOSE

In almost all fights, after a punch or a couple of kicks have been thrown, someone tries to grab, gouge, throw, grapple, or wrestle.

When the fight shifts from a long-distance to an in-close situation, the first thing you should eliminate are the punches and kicks. You cannot put maximum power into a punch or kick in close unless you are at master level in the arts. What you should be doing is striking with the forearms, elbows, and knees because that's where your striking power is greatest in close.

After you've inflicted damage with your elbow or forearm, your opponent is off-balance and he has been weakened. Now is the time for a takedown, a throw, or a grappling or locking technique. Always try to work the head and neck of your opponent because those are the easiest parts of the body to injure. He is vulnerable after you have seized his neck and head. Any way you snap, push, or twist his neck and head, his body will follow.

FIGHTING FROM A DISTANCE

During a fight you will probably at different times fight in close, at middle distance, or at long distance. If you are fighting at a long distance, you should favor traps and follow up the trapped leg or arm with a strike to the nearest vulnerable target, breaking the balance along the way. Also, the direct linear attack is safer than trying to circle when you are fighting from a distance. If your opponent counterattacks, you are in a stronger position to block or evade the hit. From that position you can easily work to his left or right side, as you are nearer to him, without putting yourself in a weak position.

I do not believe, as many systems do, in circling your opponent from the start. This is wrong because it lets your opponent quickly know before the fight starts that you have the knowledge and training to try and circle him and attack from the side or rear. You are showing him moves and directions that should come as a surprise after you are in motion, when it will be too late for him to evaluate, turn, or measure you.

THE END OF THE FIGHT

Any fight, except when you are fighting several attackers, should last less than twenty seconds. If you expect it to last longer than that, you will probably lose. After you or the opponent has made the first move and you have broken his balance, he is weak. Do not hesitate from that moment. Unload on him with hitting, kicking, felling, or grappling techniques, and it will be over very quickly.

SOME CLOSING WORDS

I began this book by saying that there is no magic to the martial arts, and there is none. But what sometimes seems magical to me is the transformation of people who take up the martial arts. Through the years I have seen hundreds of people go from unhealthy to healthy, overweight to slim, weak and slow to strong and fast, frightened to confident, shy to outgoing, all because they latched on to the martial arts and learned its discipline. The martial arts are certainly no cure-all, but for many people they are a funnel into which they can channel all the ways in which they want to improve themselves, and a vehicle for building better minds, better bodies, and better spirits. Perhaps you are one of those people.

If you do continue to pursue the martial arts, always keep in mind that the mental and physical principles are equally important. I have seen many potentially skillful fighters whose abilities never developed because they gave too much weight to one aspect of the arts and disregarded the other. Also, as you grow in the arts, be open-minded and humble. We certainly must be thankful for the precious knowledge that the ancient masters have passed on to us, and use that knowledge for good purpose. And also, as you progress, remember to search deeply within your own mind, for that is where you will find some of the greatest "secrets" of the fighting arts.

INDEX

Make Every Word Count (Provost), 55
Mantras, 29
Meditation, 27–29
Mental principles, 25–51
  attitude, 36
  beating your opponent, 47–48
  concentration, 34–35
  confidence, 37–38
  developing the mind, 18, 32–34
  eliminating emotion, 44
  eliminating fear, 40–42
  emptying your mind, 35–36
  flexibility, 31–32
  inner peace, 29–31
  meditation, 27–29
  no-mind principle, 44–46
  open-mindedness, 31–32
  patience, 38–39
  positive thinking, 39
  treatment of opponent, 46–47
    using his weaknesses, 19, 50–51
  using your strengths, 48–50
Mind, the
  development of, 18, 32–34
  emptying, 35–36
  opponent's, confusing, 164–165
Momentum, 61–62
Movement in fighting, 162–163
Movies, kung fu, 48
Mushin (no-mind), 45
Music for exercising, 104

Negative statement, positive thinking and, 39
No-mind principle, 44–46
Noncontact sparring, 149
Normal fighting stance, 160
Nose as opponent's vital spot, 74

Okinawan fighting systems, 19
Om, 29
Open-hand slash, 97
Open-mindedness, 31–32
Opponent(s)
  beating, 47–48
  body of, 42
  breaking the balance of, 164
  circling, 167
  confusing the mind of, 164–165
  ending the fight, 167
  evaluation of, 155
  immobilizing, 16
  staring at, 161
  treatment of, 46–47
  using, 33, 50–51
  vital spots to attack, 74
  weakness of, 19
  weapon of, 41

Palm heel
  forming, 125
  thrusting, 126
  willow, 127
Patience, 38–39
Peace, inner, 29–31
Physical examinations, 109
Physical principles, 53–64
  balance, 60–61
  breathing, 58
    exercises for, 58–60
  flow, 55–56
  the *kiai,* 56–57
  momentum, 61–62
  visualization, 62–64
Poison-hand techniques, 72–74
  exercises for, 119
Poking
  snake's head for, 94
  snake's tooth strike for, 96
  snake strike for, 95
  twin dragons for, 88
Positive thinking, 39
Posture for fighting, 161–162
Power, development of, 105–106
Proper fists, 123
Provost, Gary, 55, 56
Psychological weapons, 56–57
Pulling, tiger claw for, 91
Pull-ups, 106
Punching, 55
  exercises for, 105–106
  from the heel, 107
Punching for a thousand miles, 63
Push-ups, 106
  finger-tip, 119

Raking
  exercise for, 119
  tiger claw for, 91
Rationalization, 19
Reflex training, 106–107
Relaxing, 22
Reverse crescent (crescent kick), 128
Rhythmic breathing, 28
  eliminating fear by, 42
Ripping, tiger claw for, 91
Roundhouse kick, 133–135
Roundhouse knee, 83

Safety, sense of, 30
Self-confidence, 18, 19, 37–38
  inner peace and, 30
Self-defense situations, visualization of, 64
Sense of satisfaction, 30
Shaolin, 21
  dragon as symbol of heaven in, 86

INDEX

INDEX